MICROWAVE
DOUGH
CRAFT

MICROWAVE DOUGH CRAFT

MORE THAN 50 ORIGINAL SALT DOUGH PROJECTS

ALISON JENKINS

CHARTWELL
BOOKS, INC.

To Fiona, Gerry and Rob
A.J.

A QUINTET BOOK

Published by Chartwell Books
A Division of Book Sales, Inc.
114 Northfield Avenue
Edison, New Jersey 08837

This edition produced for sale in the U.S.A., its
territories and dependencies only.

ISBN 0-7858-0631-8

This book was designed and produced by
Quintet Publishing Limited
6 Blundell Street
London N7 9BH

Creative Director: Richard Dewing
Designer: Ian Hunt
Project Editor: Alison Bravington
Editor: Alison Leach
Photographer: Paul Forrester
Illustrator: Wendy Thompson

Typeset in Great Britain by
Central Southern Typsetters, Eastbourne
Manufactured in Malaysia by
C.H. Colourscan Sdn. Bhd.
Printed in Singapore by
Star Standard Industries (Pte) Ltd

CONTENTS

PROJECTS

INTRODUCTION

The use of salt dough as a modeling medium has enjoyed an enormous increase in popularity over the past few years. Although its use is widely recognized as a folk art form throughout Europe and the USA, modeling with dough has far older origins. It is believed that the Ancient Egyptians, Greeks and Romans shared the tradition of offering baked bread dough models as tributes to their Gods. In a sense that tradition is still followed – many people are familiar with the bread wheatsheaves frequently displayed at Easter. Salt dough in the form we know today evolved in Europe during the nineteenth century as a progression from traditional bread doughs, the salt being added to protect models and decorations from being eaten by vermin.

Children and adults alike can enjoy a truly satisfying creative experience, using a material that is easily manipulated, highly versatile, inexpensive and non-toxic, to produce with a little imagination a limitless variety of durable models and decorations. The beauty of salt dough lies in its simplicity: the basic materials of flour, salt and water are readily available in most kitchens. Indeed all the projects featured in this book can be created at the kitchen table using only the most basic equipment.

Traditional dough craft methods involve the models being dried by baking in a conventional oven. While the results are undoubtedly successful, it may take up to 12 to 14 hours for a larger dough piece to be dry enough to paint. Using a microwave oven dramatically reduces the baking time; for example, a small piece can take mere minutes to dry while a larger one might take only a couple of hours or less. Although microwave dough craft could not be described as "instant" and still needs a certain amount of patience, the relative speed with which models can be created and finished is a definite advantage.

The ability to produce successful craft projects using a microwave oven requires a certain understanding of how this works. What then is the difference between a conventional oven and a microwave? Basically, in a conventional oven heat is generated outside the item to be cooked and is transferred through the container to the item; in a microwave oven the heat is generated from within the item itself. Microwaves are produced by a high frequency tube called a magnetron which is usually positioned at the top of the oven. The magnetron converts electrical energy into microwaves which are passed into the oven cavity and distributed evenly by a rotating fan. The microwaves are then reflected off the metal interior of the oven back to the item to be baked.

Salt dough and all foodstuffs contain moisture. When the moisture molecules are exposed to microwaves, they begin to oscillate at 2.5 thousand million times per second. This rapid vibration causes friction which in turn generates heat. This begins around the outside and slowly penetrates to the center. Smaller thinner items will therefore bake more quickly than larger thicker ones with a greater volume of dough. The understanding of this general principle will be invaluable when working with salt dough. All microwave ovens are different and a certain amount of experimentation will be required to produce successful results; the general rule is to err on the gentle side using lower power settings at first, thus giving much more room for error.

The projects in this book fall into three basic categories, each requiring different skill levels and techniques, beginning with simple templates and flat shapes, then progressing to more complicated molding and modeling, providing instruction for the beginner and inspiration for the more experienced. Basic requirements, methods and techniques are described in the first chapter, followed by over 50 projects, each including a comprehensive equipment list and full step-by-step instructions.

EQUIPMENT
BASIC EQUIPMENT FOR TEMPLATES AND FLAT SHAPES

FLOUR Use for kneading and for sprinkling over the pastry board and rolling pin to prevent the dough from sticking.

PASTRY BOARD A wooden one is best for rolling out dough.

ROLLING PIN Use for rolling out the dough to an even thickness.

PASTRY BRUSH Use to moisten the surface of the dough with water ready to attach other flat shapes or details.

SMALL KNIFE Use to cut out simple shapes and around templates.

SCISSORS Use to cut out paper templates.

METAL CUTTERS The vast assortment of cookie,

canapé and cake decorating cutters now available are invaluable for dough craft, especially for cutting out small or intricate shapes.

MODELING TOOLS These plastic tools have pointed, blunt and rounded ends and blades are readily available from craft supply stores and are useful for cutting out fine shapes, smoothing out dough, making surface patterns and indentations.

WOODEN SKEWERS Use for making surface patterns and applying adhesive.

PAPER AND TRACING PAPER Use for tracing and cutting templates.

PENCIL Use for tracing templates and sketching.

BASIC EQUIPMENT FOR MOLDING AND MODELING

ASSORTED MOLDS Use microwave-safe dishes, plates and bowls as molds; other objects such as egg shells and bottles can be used.

CARD AND CARD MOLDS Make your own molds from thin card.

PLASTIC FOOD WRAP An essential item when molding salt dough: a layer of plastic food wrap stretched over the mold will prevent the dough from sticking.

KNIFE Use for trimming edges of molded shapes and for cutting out small shapes.

MODELING TOOLS An assortment of plastic tools each differently shaped for cutting, modeling and surface decoration.

FORK The tines of a fork make even grooves when pressed into the surface of raw dough.

GARLIC PRESS Use to create texture.

MODELING SYRINGE This has a number of different fittings enabling different shaped strands of dough to be extruded.

WOODEN SKEWERS AND TOOTHPICKS Use to create surface textures, apply adhesive and support small objects like beads for baking and painting.

SHELLS OR OTHER THREE-DIMENSIONAL OBJECTS Many objects can be used to emboss surface patterns – simply press the shape firmly onto the surface of the raw dough.

FABRIC Use for backings for small pictures.

WIRE Bend short lengths of wire into decorative shapes and use for embossing patterns into raw dough.

METAL CUTTERS Collect a variety of metal cutters to cut out flower petals, leaves, letters and other small shapes.

ADHESIVE TAPE Use masking tape to join card molds together and double-sided tape for holding small shapes in position for painting.

FLORIST'S FOAM Press salt dough beads onto toothpicks and stick into florist's foam while the beads are being painted.

BASIC EQUIPMENT FOR PAINTING
AND FINISHING

ACRYLIC CRAFT PAINTS AND SPRAY PAINT Non-water-based acrylic craft paints are ideal for decorating dough pieces as they provide good color coverage and are quick drying.

OIL PAINT Use together with crackle varnish.

PAINTBRUSHES An assortment of different sized paintbrushes for applying paint and varnish.

TOOTHBRUSH Use to create a speckled paint effect.

SPONGES Use natural and synthetic sponges to produce a mottled paint effect.

POLYURETHANE VARNISH Available in gloss, matt and satin finishes; use to seal and protect finished dough pieces.

CRACKLE VARNISH A specialty varnish used to create an antique, crackled look.

QUICK-DRYING CRAFT ADHESIVE Use for fixing small light items such as beads to dough models.

EPOXY RESIN ADHESIVE Use this strong adhesive for repair work, for attaching small features to larger dough pieces and for fixing metal fittings.

STENCIL FILM Use this transparent plastic film for making stencils.

CRAFT KNIFE OR SCALPEL Use for cutting out stencils.

SANDPAPER Use fine grade sandpaper for smoothing rough edges and corners of baked dough pieces in preparation for decoration.

WIRE Bend short lengths of wire into decorative shapes for embossing; use finer wire for holding shapes together.

STRING AND RAFFIA Use to make decorative hanging loops for Christmas decorations and small pictures, and for attaching small dough pieces.

LEAVES The underside of a large leaf makes a delicate embossed pattern when pressed into the surface of raw dough.

NEEDLES AND SEWING THREAD Use for general sewing and attaching beads.

BEADS Use for embellishments and for Christmas decorations.

METAL FITTINGS Fittings such as magnets, jewelry findings, metal brackets, and brooch clasps are fixed to the painted models with epoxy resin adhesive.

MAKING AND BAKING SALT DOUGH

This chapter contains the basic salt dough recipe which has been used for every project in this book, and general guidelines to the preparation, baking and care of finished dough pieces. There are many recipes for salt dough, each requiring different proportions of flour to salt, and some including vegetable oil or wallpaper paste. However, this is the simplest recipe of all, and after much experimentation I have found it to be the most successful. For smaller amounts of dough, simply decrease your measure or for a larger amount increase the quantities, keeping the same proportions. Use regular all-purpose flour, not self rising, as the rising agents will puff up during the baking process ruining your models, and use any finely granulated table salt. One cup of water is usually sufficient to bind the dry ingredients together. As you become more experienced, you will be able to judge exactly how much is required, perhaps a little more or a little less.

MAKING THE SALT DOUGH

INGREDIENTS
3 cups all-purpose flour
1 cup fine table salt
1 cup cold water

EQUIPMENT
Mixing bowl
Measuring pitcher
Mixing spoon
Wooden pastry board
Plastic bag

Mix the flour and the salt together thoroughly with a spoon in a large bowl and then gradually add the cold water. Continue mixing until the contents of the bowl resemble a rough dough. Remove the dough from the bowl and knead thoroughly on a lightly floured pastry board for about 10 minutes until it is smooth and elastic and slightly warm to the touch.

Place the dough in a plastic bag to rest for about an hour. The dough can then be rolled out flat on a lightly floured wooden pastry board, molded or modeled as the project requires.

TIPS
• Take care not to add too much water when making the dough as it will become too sticky and difficult to use.
• Salt dough will keep for about a week if placed in an airtight container or a sealed plastic bag inside the refrigerator. Always knead the dough again thoroughly on a floured pastry board after it has been in the refrigerator so it becomes soft and elastic again.
• Make sure that the rolling pin and pastry board are floured to prevent the dough from sticking. Always use all-purpose flour, never self rising.

BAKING THE SALT DOUGH

When the dough piece has been completed, transfer it to the microwave oven for baking. If the piece has been made on a properly floured pastry board, it can be slid directly onto the turntable plate inside the oven, or, alternatively, carefully lifted using your hands, a spatula or a knife with a large flat blade. Place molded and modeled pieces in the center of the turntable plate; smaller pieces can be arranged evenly around the edge. Baking times vary greatly depending on the size, shape and thickness of the individual piece. Smaller thinner pieces generally cook more quickly than larger thicker ones. Surface area is also a contributory factor in

determining baking times. For example, you will find that a modeled piece with many small parts like leaves or flowers will dry out more quickly than one with a larger volume of dough but a smaller surface area such as a bowl or a large flat plaque.

As a rule, begin baking slowly on the lowest possible power setting and as you increase the power, decrease the baking time. Using a high power setting first will cause the model to swell and crack. Power output varies from model to model. Most microwave ovens are 650 or 850 watts. An 850-watt model was used for testing all the projects in this book. It is not usually necessary to use power settings higher than medium for baking salt dough. Baking times have been calculated on the following basis:

low:	80 watts
medium low:	150 watts
medium:	300 watts
medium high:	450 watts
high:	600 watts
full:	850 watts

Check the instruction manual of your microwave oven to assess which settings match the guidelines given here. A certain amount of experimentation may be necessary to discover how best to use your microwave oven.

Here is an example of the baking sequences suggested throughout the book: low for 20 minutes + 20 minutes, medium low for 10 minutes + 10 minutes, and medium for 5 minutes + 5 minutes. This means bake on low power for 20 minutes, leave to rest for a few minutes, and then bake again for an additional 20 minutes. Increase the power to medium low. Bake for 10 minutes, leave to rest for a few minutes, and then bake for an additional 10 minutes. Finally, increase the power to medium. Bake for 5 minutes, leave to rest for a few minutes, and then bake for an additional 5 minutes. By this time the piece should be dry enough, but if not, just leave to rest, then return to the microwave oven and repeat the last baking sequence.

Never leave the microwave oven unattended while baking is in progress because salt dough can scorch easily. Check the model at regular intervals, and allow a few minutes "rest" between baking periods. Remember that the dough will continue to dry out as it cools. If the dough begins to bubble or swell, stop the cooking process and let the piece rest. Then begin again.

When the dough is dry, it should be hard and crisp. Turn the model over and tap the underside with your index finger – it should sound hollow; if not, return the model to the microwave oven and repeat the last baking period until it is completely dry. It is easy to tell if a molded shape is ready because the dough shrinks away slightly from the mold when dry. After the baking process is complete, remove the model and leave to cool completely before sanding and decorating. Do not attempt to remove a mold while the dough is still warm. Without the support of the mold the shape may warp as it cools.

TIPS
• If your model cracks slightly during the baking process, don't panic, just repair the damage by smoothing on a little fresh dough and then rebake to dry. Another method is to cover cracks or level out uneven surfaces using a light colored wood filler – this will dry naturally without the use of the microwave oven. The repairs can be sanded down smoothly in the usual way. Other breakages can be repaired by using a strong epoxy resin adhesive.

SAFETY NOTES
• Always remember to use pot holders when removing baked items from the microwave. Both the dough and the molds can become very hot; also some items can give off steam which can burn your skin.
• Do not place metal containers or those with metal parts in the microwave oven as this may cause arcing which can damage the oven or cause a fire. Always make sure that any molds used are microwave-safe. Tempered glass, ceramic, wood, microwave-safe plastics, rubber and cardboard are all considered suitable for use in the microwave oven. To test the suitability of a container, half fill with cold water and cook on high power for about 1 minute. If the water is hot and the container remains cool, then it is safe to use.

TECHNIQUES

The projects contained in this chapter serve as an introduction to dough craft, providing an excellent opportunity to develop skills and to practice decorative paint finishes.

——— TEMPLATES AND FLAT SHAPES ———

The beginner will find the use of simple templates and cutters an easy way to get started, as they help you to learn how to handle dough and to become familiar with using the microwave oven. Templates also form the basis of some of the more complicated projects featured later in the book. All the relevant templates needed for each project are included on pages 116–127. Trace off the outline and any decorative details onto a piece of plain paper, then cut out the design with a pair of sharp scissors.

1 Knead a ball of dough on a lightly floured pastry board. Using a floured rolling pin, roll out a thickness of approximately ¼ inch and place the paper template on top of the dough. Cut out and remove the inner areas first, using a small modeling knife, then cut around the template roughly with a larger knife. Carefully remove the waste dough from around the shape, place it in a plastic bag, and store in the refrigerator for future use.

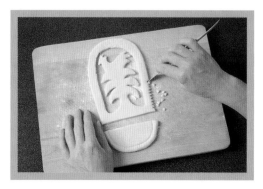

2 Use a small modeling tool to cut away small areas and to create finer details. Any surface details or decorations can be applied at this stage.

TIPS
• To create a rounded edge, press either your finger or a flat modeling tool along the edge of the dough.
• Flat shapes, sausage shapes and small details can be joined to the main piece by first moistening the surface with a little water to make it tacky, using your finger or a pastry brush for this. The two pieces can be pressed together. Smooth out the join with a modeling tool if necessary.
• The application of surface textures or indentations is not only decorative but aids the drying process by increasing the surface area, and also helps to keep pieces flat during baking. Make any holes for hanging loops and so on before the piece is baked. Pierce the dough with a wooden skewer or a toothpick.

MOLDING

With a little imagination an enormous variety of exciting decorative bowls, plates and containers can be made using everyday objects as molds. Almost anything can be used providing it is microwave safe, from a ceramic plate to an eggshell. And if you cannot find a suitable mold, just make your own from thin card. All the projects featuring card molds have trace-off templates (see pages 116–127). The salt dough form can be created in two ways: molding a flat dough piece or cutout shape, or building up the shape with sausage-shaped coils. Decorative or functional details such as rims, handles, bases, lids, relief and embossed patterns can be added to create imaginative and original pieces to keep yourself or for gifts.

MOLDING OVER A BOWL

1 First cover the outside of the bowl with a layer of transparent plastic food wrap – this will prevent the dough from sticking to the mold. Roll out a quantity of dough to about ¼-inch thickness on a lightly floured pastry board. Lift the dough carefully, supporting it underneath with your hand, and place over the inverted bowl. Press the dough gently down the sides of the bowl with your hands so it lies flat. Make sure that the dough is not too wet as it may stretch when lifted.

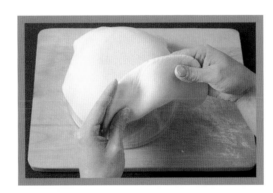

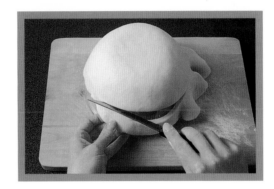

2 Trim the edge level with a small sharp knife. Press the blade of the knife gently against the edge of the dough after it has been trimmed to make a smooth edge. You can make a rounded edge by pressing your fingers along the cut edge.

MOLDING OVER AN EGG

Roll out a small quantity of dough on a lightly floured pastry board to about ¼-inch thickness. Cut out a large star-shape using a cookie cutter. Place the cut dough shape over an egg and smooth the points down each side.

1 Trace off the required template and cut out the shape in light flexible card. Bend the flat shapes to form tapered tubes or cones and fix together with double-sided tape and masking tape. Do not use staples, as metal objects cannot be placed in the microwave oven. Attach bottoms to the card shapes with tabs of masking tape.

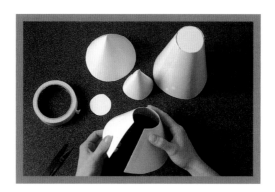

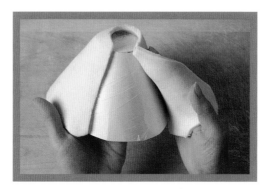

2 Cover the card mold with a layer of transparent plastic food wrap to prevent the dough sticking. Roll out a quantity of dough on a floured pastry board to about ¼-inch thickness. Place the original tracing on top and cut around it, using a sharp knife. Discard the excess dough, then carefully lift the shape, and wrap it around the card mold.

3 Press the edges of the dough together smoothly across the bottom of the mold and along the join at the side. Trim the edge level with a small sharp knife and then smooth off the cut edge.

1 Cover the mold with a layer of transparent plastic food wrap. Roll a ball of well-kneaded dough into sausages about ⅝ inch in diameter. Beginning at the bottom of the mold, wind the sausage around, pressing slightly to the surface of the mold. Join on new sausages as you go.

2 Using a rounded modeling tool moistened with a little water, carefully smooth all the joins between the coils. This insures that the coiled shape stays together during the cooking process and also makes an interesting surface texture.

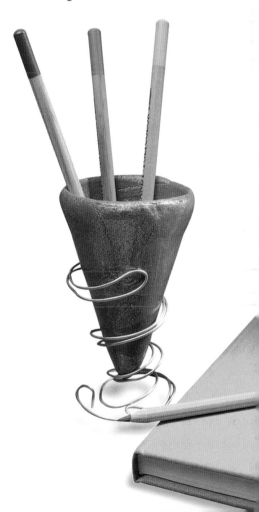

1 Use a small bowl as a mold for both pieces. First mold, trim and bake a plain bowl shape. (See Molding over a bowl, page 15.) Remove the dough shape from the mold and set aside – this will form the lower section of the bowl.

2 Using the same mold, repeat the process but this time cut away a round of dough at the bottom of the mold (this will be the opening of the bowl). Roll out a sausage of dough about ⅝ inch in diameter and approximately long enough to fit around the cutout section (this will form the rim of the bowl). Use a modeling tool or small knife, cut the ends of the sausage diagonally so they will fit together neatly. Moisten the edge of the cutout section with water and press the rim in place.

3 Place the sausage around the cutout section, gently pressing into place. Make sure that the diagonally cut ends fit together neatly.

4 Using a modeling tool moistened with water, carefully smooth out the join between the rim and the bowl. Bake this upper section and then remove from the mold.

5 Place the two baked sections together and press small balls of raw dough over the join on the inside and the outside. Smooth out the raw dough with your fingers or a modeling tool moistened with water. Bake the shape again so all the dough is completely dry.

ADDING A BOTTOM TO A BOWL

Press rolled-out dough or large cutout shapes over a mold. Roll out a sausage of about ⅝ inch in diameter, and long enough to form a round at the bottom of the bowl. Use a knife or modeling tool to cut the ends diagonally so they will fit together neatly.

Moisten the surface of the dough around the bottom with a little water, then lightly press the sausage in place to form a round. Smooth out the join between the bottom and the bowl with a modeling tool moistened with water. The same method can be used to add a bottom to vases or plates.

ADDING SURFACE TEXTURES

Add fine string-like relief patterns and textures to raw dough forms by using a modeling syringe. This is a clever tool used by model-makers to extrude dough, clay, or fondant frosting. It has a number of different sized and shaped fittings. Place a small amount of well-kneaded dough in the syringe, insert the plunger, and gently depress it to extrude the dough. You can "draw" a pattern directly onto the dough shape.

A wooden skewer is an invaluable modeling tool. Use the blunt end to make circular indentations into the surface of the dough. Not only does this create a decorative effect, but it also prevents flat shapes puffing up during baking.

Add a relief pattern by cutting rounds of rolled-out dough into spirals using a small knife, then moisten the surface of the dough shape with water, and press the spirals into place. Smooth out the join with a modeling tool moistened with water, then add some decoration, using a wooden skewer. All flat dough shapes can be added to larger pieces in this way.

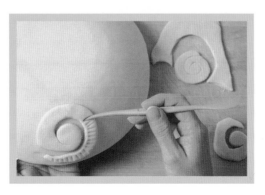

Use the underside of a large fresh leaf to emboss a pattern into the surface of a raw dough shape. The veins of the leaf will make clear indentations in the dough.

Bend a short piece of wire to form a spiral shape, leaving a small "tail" at the center to use as a handle. Press the shape into the surface of the raw dough. You can use all sorts of objects to create embossed patterns in this way – for example, keys, shells and pieces of string.

MODELING

The versatility of salt dough as a modeling medium is clearly illustrated in this chapter. Its ability to hold quite fine details makes it very well-suited to three-dimensional work of all kinds. Using your imagination and a combination of the dough craft skills and methods already described in the sections covering molding and template work, it is possible to create an astonishing variety of beautiful ornaments, frames, jewelry, and many other decorative pieces. Some projects are template-based while others involve molding and free modeling techniques. Modeling with salt dough may seem a little tricky at first but with a little patience and practice you will get used to the dough, and you will soon be able to produce amazing results.

BOWLED AND TWISTED SHAPES

Roll out a small quantity of dough on a lightly floured pastry board to about ¼-inch thickness. Cut out the basic spoon shape using the template on page 122. Use your fingers or the bowl of a teaspoon to press the edges of the cut shape into a bowl shape. Use the blunt end of a wooden skewer to add surface patterns.

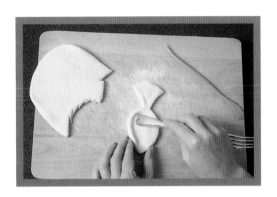

Roll out two sausage-shapes and twist together. Make sure that the ends stick together by moistening with water and then pressing with your fingers.

FREE MODELING

Create elegant swirls by first rolling out a sausage-shape tapered at both ends, then pinching the shape between your thumb and forefinger to form a pointed ridge all the way along.

Curl up the shape from one end to form the swirl. Attach to the main dough shape or cutout by moistening the surface with a little water, then gently pressing the molded piece into position.

STARFISH AND SHELLS

For a starfish, cut out a five-pointed star shape roughly, then pinch each point between your thumb and forefinger. Add surface textures with a toothpick or wooden skewer. For shells, roll out sausage-shapes tapered at one end and then roll up the shapes from the tapered end to form the shells. It is best to add the flat starfish to the model before baking, while the larger shell shapes are best baked first and then glued to the baked model using a strong epoxy resin adhesive.

LEAVES AND FLOWERS

For leaves, cut out leaf shapes using small cookie cutters or templates. Add surface texture by pressing the tines of a fork firmly into the dough or create veins by pressing the point of a modeling tool, skewer or toothpick into the surface of the raw rough. For rosebuds, cut out an oval or leaf shape using a cutter or template, and then flatten the dough between your fingers to make a larger thinner shape. Roll up the shape from one end to form a rosebud.

There are a great many small metal cutters available in flower, leaf and petal shapes, which are fun to use and very effective when combined with other surface textures. To make a large flower, roll out a quantity of dough quite thinly and cut out the required shapes. Build up the petal layers as shown. Squeeze a small quantity of dough through a garlic press to form the seeded centers of the sunflowers and daisies, scoop off the dough with a modeling knife, and lightly press the dough onto the flower shape. Using a modeling tool, wooden skewer or toothpick, press any surface details into the flowers and leaves when the dough is raw.

MAKING BEADS

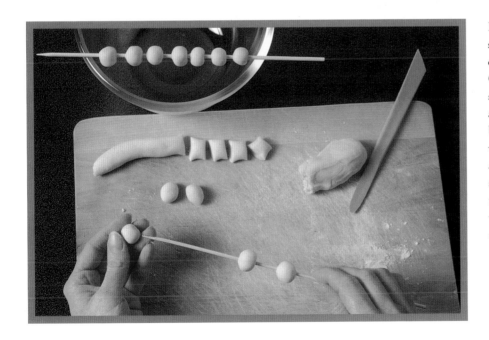

Roll a small ball of dough into a sausage-shape about the diameter of the finished bead. Cut off equal sections of the sausage with a modeling knife and roll each one into a small ball. Thread the balls onto a wooden skewer and balance across the rim of a microwave-safe bowl. The beads can bake in the microwave oven in this way without distorting their rounded shape.

FINISHING, PAINTING, AND
DECORATIVE EFFECTS

After the baking process is completed, the salt dough pieces are ready for finishing and decoration. Most will benefit from an undercoat of acrylic paint in a neutral or matching color as a base for more decorative paintwork and also to act as a sealant. How you decorate the dough pieces is an entirely personal choice. Flat shapes lend themselves well to sponging, freehand patterns and crackle varnish finishes, while more realistic or three-dimensional shapes require more detailed paintwork. Take this opportunity to experiment using different colors and the techniques described. The advantage of using acrylic paints is that if you make a mistake or are dissatisfied with the finished result, you can simply repaint with a base color and start again. Also, acrylic paints are non-water-based, so reabsorption of moisture is minimized. When all the decorative paintwork has dried thoroughly, the entire model must be sealed with three or more coats of a polyurethane varnish; this is crucial as the varnish protects the dough from reabsorption of moisture.

Most dough pieces require a little sanding or smoothing after baking. Lightly rub a fine grade sandpaper over straight edges and flat surfaces to prepare the surface for painting and even out any roughness. Use a smaller piece for more intricate areas.

After sanding, all salt dough pieces will benefit from a base coat of emulsion paint or acrylic craft paint. This acts as a sealant and creates a better surface for decorative effects. Sponging is an excellent method of paint application as the surface of the dough tends to be a little uneven. Simply spread a little paint onto a palette or saucer, dip the sponge into the paint, and then press lightly onto the dough piece. Experiment a little with several colors or with metallic paints. A natural sponge will give an irregular mottled effect, while the use of a synthetic sponge will result in a more even, smaller pattern.

IMPORTANT NOTE
Although the dough shapes will be completely sealed with acrylic paints and three coats of varnish and are relatively waterproof, do not fill with or immerse in water or liquid of any kind. Dough pieces may, however, be wiped clean with a damp cloth.
As reabsorption of moisture would ruin a salt dough model it is advisable not to keep or hang them in damp or steamy places such as a bathroom or above a stove in a kitchen. Salt dough decorations are not suitable for outdoor use.

Use an old toothbrush dipped in paint mixed to a watery consistency to create a fine speckled effect. Aim the brush at the dough piece and then draw the blade of a knife toward you. Small spots of paint will be deposited on the surface of the dough piece. This decorative effect results in an almost stone-like appearance.

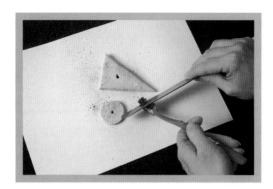

Using leaves as stencils is an easy way of decorating a flat plate. Place the leaf in the center of the plate and then apply a lighter colored paint all around it, using a small synthetic sponge. When the leaf is removed, the shape will be left in negative.

Crackle varnish gives an attractive antiqued look to flat dough pieces. The varnish is usually sold as a kit with two pots of varnish plus instructions.

1 Apply the first step varnish to the dough shape and leave to dry for 20–30 minutes. Then apply the second step varnish and leave to dry. As the second step varnish dries, you will see the cracks begin to appear.

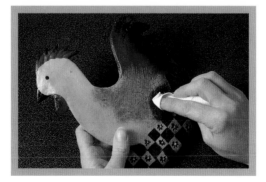

2 When the second step varnish has dried completely and the entire surface is cracked, rub a small amount of burnt umber oil paint into the cracks with a soft cloth. This accentuates the cracks and adds to the antique effect.

1
TEMPLATES
AND
CUTTERS

Rustic Chicken

Add a touch of country charm to your kitchen wall with this two-dimensional chicken. Subtle earthy colors and a crackle varnish finish make for an authentic rustic look. Mounted on a small block of wood, the chicken can be hung on a wall or used as a freestanding ornament on a shelf.

YOU WILL NEED

½ batch salt dough (see page 11)
Rolling pin
Flour
Pastry board
Tracing paper
Pencil
Scissors
Small knife
Fine grade sandpaper
Paint brushes
Acrylic paints
Satin polyurethane varnish
Crackle varnish kit
Burnt umber oil paint
Soft cloth
Block of wood
    about 3 x 1¼ x ½ inches
Epoxy resin adhesive

● Roll out the dough to a thickness of ¼ inch on a lightly floured pastry board.

● Trace off the chicken template on page 116. Cut out the template and lay it on top of the rolled-out dough. Use a small knife to cut around the outside of the template.

● Transfer the dough shape to the microwave turntable plate and bake on low for 20 minutes + 20 minutes, medium low for 10 minutes + 10 minutes + 10 minutes, and medium for 5 minutes + 5 minutes + 5 minutes. Remove from the microwave oven and let cool before painting. Using sandpaper, smooth away any rough edges or corners.

● Apply two coats of a beige-colored base paint to both sides of the chicken, letting each coat dry before applying the next. Then paint on the decorative features, using the photograph as a guide.

● Apply three coats of satin varnish to the reverse side of the chicken and leave to dry. When the varnish has dried, turn the chicken over and apply the first step of the crackle varnish. Leave to dry for 30 minutes and then apply the second step. When the surface is completely dry and well crackled, rub in some burnt umber oil paint with a soft cloth (see page 25).

● Using epoxy resin glue, attach the block of wood to the reverse side of the chicken, positioning the block flush with the lower edge of the chicken so it can be freestanding if required.

Cupid's Arrows

Inspired by a nineteenth-century American weathervane, this romantic wall decoration would make a charming good luck token for a bride or perhaps a housewarming gift.

YOU WILL NEED

¼ batch salt dough (see page 11)
Rolling pin
Flour
Pastry board
Tracing paper
Pencil
Scissors
Modeling knife
Small knife
Toothpick
Bodkin
Fine grade sandpaper
Paintbrushes
Acrylic paints
Silver metallic paint
Sponge
Satin polyurethane varnish
20 inches matching ribbon

● Roll out the dough to a thickness of ¼ inch on a lightly floured pastry board.

● Trace off the heart and arrows template on page 117. Cut out the paper template and lay it on top of the rolled-out dough.

● Begin by using the modeling knife to cut out the small sections between the arrow shafts, then cut around the outside of the template, using the small knife. Remove the paper template and mark the lines on the arrows by lightly running the point of a toothpick along the surface of the dough. Then pierce two holes at the top of the heart, using a bodkin.

● Transfer to microwave turntable plate and bake on low for 20 minutes + 20 minutes, medium low for 10 minutes + 10 minutes, and medium for 5 minutes. Remove from the microwave oven and let cool before painting. Using the sandpaper, smooth away any rough edges.

● Paint the heart a sunny yellow color and the arrows sky blue. When the paint has dried, decorate the heart with a central motif surrounded by dots or stripes. Use your imagination to create your own design motifs, or perhaps incorporate a short message or greeting. Sponge some silver metallic paint on the arrows to add a little sparkle.

● When the paint has dried thoroughly, apply three coats of satin varnish, letting each coat dry before applying the next.

● Finally, cut the ribbon in half and thread one half through each of the holes at the top of the shape. Tie in a knot and trim the ends neatly.

Creative Cards

Everyone loves to receive a handmade greetings card, it makes the occasion so much more personal and special. Tiny canapé and cookie cutters were used to make these heart, star and triangular dough shapes but you could experiment a little with your own designs and templates.

YOU WILL NEED

Small amount of salt dough (see
    page 11). You can use waste
    dough from other projects
Rolling pin
Flour
Pastry board
Assorted canapé or small
    cookie cutters
Bodkin
Fine grade sandpaper
Paintbrushes
Acrylic paints
Satin polyurethane varnish
Pencil
Scissors
Thin colored card or
    handmade paper
Scalpel
Metal ruler
Leather punch
Fine string
Double-sided adhesive tape or
    double-sided adhesive pads

NOTE
• Cards with salt dough
motifs may be a little
heavier than regular cards.
Bear this in mind if you
want to send your
greetings by mail.

● Roll out the dough to a thickness of ⅛ inch on a lightly floured pastry board.

● Stamp out the heart, star and triangular shapes, using canapé or small cookie cutters. Use a bodkin to pierce two holes in the center of the shapes that are to be tied on with string.

● Transfer the shapes to the microwave turntable plate and bake on low for 10 minutes, medium low for 5 minutes, and medium for 2 minutes. Remove the shapes from the microwave oven and leave to cool. Using sandpaper, smooth off any rough edges before painting.

● Paint the shapes on both sides with acrylic paint. When dry, apply a coat of satin varnish to both sides and leave to dry.

● Cut the card or paper into 4- x 8-inch rectangles. Fold in half widthways to form square cards. Attach a square or small patch of contrasting or handmade paper to the front of each card. Cut out small windows in some, using a scalpel and metal ruler. Use a leather punch to create a row of decorative holes around the edge. Tie the pierced shapes to the cards with short lengths of fine string. Attach the dough motifs in the windows with double-sided adhesive tape or double-sided adhesive pads for a more three-dimensional effect.

Folk Art Gift Tags

*Gingerbread men and folk art fish make delightful gift tags, each one with a
heart-shaped cutout. Using cookie cutters and a simple template, this project is
ideal for beginners.*

YOU WILL NEED

¼ batch salt dough (see page 11)
    makes about four of each shape
Rolling pin
Flour
Pastry board
Gingerbread men cookie cutters
Small heart-shaped canapé cutter
Tracing paper
Pencil
Scissors
Small knife or modeling knife
Bodkin or toothpick
Fine grade sandpaper
Paintbrushes
Acrylic paints
Satin polyurethane varnish
Natural raffia
Small squares of colored paper
Double-sided adhesive tape

● Roll out the dough to a thickness of ¼ inch on a well-floured pastry board. Use the cookie cutters to press out the gingerbread shapes, and then the canapé cutter for the heart shape.

● Trace off the fish template on page 116 (there are two sizes to choose from). Cut out as many paper shapes as you need and lay them on the rolled-out dough. Use a small knife or a modeling knife to cut carefully around the templates.

● Using a bodkin or toothpick, pierce a small hole at the top of each shape and transfer them to the microwave turntable plate. Bake in batches of 6 or 8 at a time on low for 20 minutes + 20 minutes and medium low for 10 minutes + 10 minutes. Remove the baked shapes from the microwave oven and leave to cool. Using sandpaper, smooth off any rough edges or corners.

● Apply two coats of acrylic paint to each side of the gift tags, letting each coat dry before applying the next. To finish and seal, apply three coats of satin varnish, letting each coat dry before applying the next.

● Thread a short length of raffia through the hole in each gift tag. Write a message on a small square of colored paper and attach to the reverse of each tag with double-sided adhesive tape. Tie the tags to the packages with tiny bows.

Palm Tree Mirror Frames

These chunky mirror frames make fun wall decorations. The unusual shape is enhanced by a bold green and blue color scheme. Use a natural sponge to achieve the random mottled effect.

YOU WILL NEED

½ batch salt dough (see page 11)
    makes two mirror frames
Rolling pin
Flour
Pastry board
Tracing paper
Pencil
Scissors
Small knife
Fine grade sandpaper
Paintbrushes
Acrylic paints
Mixing palette
Small natural sponge
Satin polyurethane varnish
Two small purse-size mirrors,
    approximately 2 x 3¼ inches
Epoxy resin adhesive
Two pieces of card for backing,
    approximately 2¾ x 4 inches
    each
Double-sided adhesive pads
Self-adhesive plate hanger

● Roll out the dough to a thickness of ⅜ inch on a lightly floured pastry board. Trace off the mirror template on page 117. Cut out two shapes and place on top of the rolled-out dough. Cut out and remove the rectangular "window" at the center of each frame, then carefully cut around the outside edge.

● One at a time, transfer the frames to the microwave turntable plate and bake on low for 30 minutes + 30 minutes, medium low for 15 minutes + 15 minutes + 15 minutes, and medium for 5 minutes + 5 minutes. Remove the frames from the microwave oven and leave to cool before painting. Using sandpaper, smooth off any rough edges, paying close attention to the points.

● Apply two coats of acrylic paint to both sides of the frames, painting one blue and the other green. Spread a little green paint onto a mixing palette, dip a small natural sponge into the paint, and press the surface of the sponge onto the blue frame. The naturally irregular holes in the sponge leave a random mottled impression. Continue until the frame is covered with the pattern. Decorate the green frame in the same way but using blue paint.

● When the paint is dry, apply three coats of satin varnish to both sides of each frame, letting each coat dry before applying the next.

● Attach the mirror to the center of the card backing, using epoxy resin adhesive. When the glue is dry, use double-sided adhesive pads to attach the card to the reverse side of the mirror frame. The mirrors can be hung up by using self-adhesive plate hangers, the type used to hang china plates.

Teapot Refrigerator Magnets

*Keep your messages and reminders firmly in place on your refrigerator door
with these cute little teapot magnets. Copy the decorative ideas shown here or
paint some to match the color scheme in your kitchen or even to match
your favorite china.*

YOU WILL NEED

¼ batch salt dough (see page 11)

Rolling pin

Flour

Pastry board

Tracing paper

Pencil

Scissors

Small knife

Modeling knife

Fine grade sandpaper

Paintbrushes

Acrylic paint

Satin polyurethane varnish

Small magnets

Epoxy resin adhesive

● Roll out the dough to a thickness of ¼ inch on a lightly floured pastry board. Trace off the teapot template on page 117 three times. Cut out the templates and place each one on top of the rolled-out dough. Using a small knife, cut roughly around each template. Then using a smaller modeling knife, carefully cut out and remove the dough section inside the handle. Cut more accurately around the outside and then remove the template.

● Roll a small ball of dough into a sausage about ¼ inch in diameter. Cut one 2-inch long piece for the upper rim and another 2¾-inch long piece for the bottom. Moisten the area around the bottom and rim on the teapot shapes (these are indicated with dotted lines on the template). Use your fingers to round off the ends of the cut pieces and then gently press into position. Roll a small ball of dough for the knob on the lid and gently press into position.

● Transfer the teapot shapes to the microwave turntable plate and bake on low for 15 minutes + 15 minutes, medium low for 10 minutes + 10 minutes, and medium for 5 minutes + 5 minutes. Remove from the microwave oven and leave to cool before painting. Using sandpaper, smooth off any rough areas.

● Apply two coats of white acrylic paint to both sides of the teapot and leave to dry. Then paint on the colored details, using your imagination or the photograph as a guide. Apply three coats of satin varnish, leaving each coat to dry before applying the next. Remember to varnish both sides of the dough piece.

● Attach a small magnet to the reverse side of each teapot, using epoxy resin adhesive.

Noughts and Crosses

An entertaining gift for a child or adult, a noughts and crosses game that can be played time and time again without the need for pencil and paper. Each square salt dough counter has a nought or a cross stamped out of it with a small cookie cutter.

YOU WILL NEED

¼ batch salt dough (see page 11)

Rolling pin

Flour

Pastry board

Small knife

Alphabet cookie cutters, "O" and "X"

Fine grade sandpaper

Paintbrushes

Acrylic paints

Satin polyurethane varnish

Small wooden box to hold the counters

TIP
Alphabet or counting games can be made in the same way using dough counters and cookie cutters as an entertaining and educational toy for a child.

● Roll out the dough to a thickness of ¼ inch on a lightly floured pastry board. Cut the dough into ten 1½-inch squares. (You can make the counters larger if required – it is a good idea to find a suitable box first and then make the counters to fit.) Using cookie cutters, stamp out five "O's" and five "X's" from the dough squares.

● Transfer the counters to the microwave turntable plate and bake on low for 10 minutes + 10 minutes, medium low for 5 minutes + 5 minutes, and medium for 2 minutes + 2 minutes. Remove the baked counters from the microwave oven and leave to cool. Using sandpaper, smooth off any rough edges before painting.

● Paint the counters on both sides with acrylic paint. Make the noughts and crosses different colors. When the paint is dry, apply three coats of satin varnish to both sides, letting each coat dry before applying the next.

● If you have a plain wooden box like this one, mix some paint to a watery consistency and apply a wash of color to the wood so it matches the painted counters.

Terracotta Earrings

These striking clip-on earrings are made from simple dough shapes joined together with brass curtain rings. They are easy to make, and can be colored to coordinate with your outfit.

YOU WILL NEED

small batch salt dough
   (see page 11)
Rolling pin
Flour
Pastry board
Tracing paper
Pencil
Scissors
Small knife
Small round canapé cutter
Fine grade sandpaper
Paintbrushes
Acrylic paint
Gold metallic acrylic paint
Satin polyurethane varnish
Four small curtain rings about
   ½ inch in diameter
Wire cutter (you will need this to
   cut the curtain rings if they are
   not already split)
Two earring clip fastenings for
   each pair
Epoxy resin adhesive

● Roll out the dough to a thickness of ¼ inch on a lightly floured pastry board. Trace off the earring templates on page 118 (you will need to cut out two templates to make a pair). As they are asymmetrically shaped, you will need to reverse the second template. Cut around the template using a small knife, take the small round canapé cutter and cut out the holes where indicated.

● Transfer the earrings to the microwave turntable plate and bake on low for 10 minutes, medium low 5 minutes, and medium for 2 minutes. Remove the earrings from the microwave oven and leave to cool. Using sandpaper, smooth off any rough areas.

● Paint the earrings on both sides with a base color and leave to dry. Then take a small amount of a contrasting color paint on the end of your forefinger and rub lightly over the painted surface on both sides. Do the same with a gold metallic paint. As the surface of baked salt dough is usually uneven, this will give an interesting effect.

● Apply three coats of satin varnish to both sides of the painted earrings, letting each coat dry before applying the next.

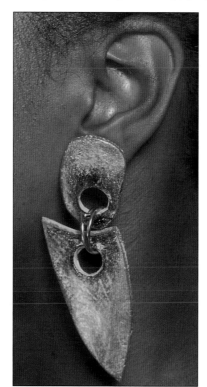

● Join the two halves of each earring together with two brass curtain rings. If you cannot find any that are already split, just snip with the point of a wire cutter. Squeeze the rings closed when the two halves are joined.

● Attach a clip fastening to the reverse side of each earring, using epoxy resin adhesive.

Starlight Candle Holders

Star-shaped candle holders richly decorated with gold paint and tiny golden beads will add a special tough to the dinner table. Group them together as a centerpiece or make individual ones for each of your guests.

YOU WILL NEED

½ batch salt dough (see page 11)

Rolling pin

Flour

Pastry board

Tracing paper

Pencil

Scissors

Small knife

Wooden skewer

Fine grade sandpaper

Paintbrushes

Acrylic paint

Gold metallic acrylic paint

Quick-drying craft glue

Tiny gold beads

Satin polyurethane varnish

Small candles (room-scenter type
    are ideal)

SAFETY NOTE
• Never leave burning candles unattended. Always place candles on a heat-resistant surface and do not let candles burn down too low.

● Roll out the dough to a thickness of ½ inch on a lightly floured pastry board. Trace off the candle holder template on page 117 (scale up the outline on a photocopying machine to make a larger one). Cut out as many templates as you require and lay each one on the rolled-out dough. Cut around each shape roughly with a small knife and then carefully cut out the center round. Cut more accurately around the template and remove the paper.

● Using the blunt end of a wooden skewer, make indentations around the edge of the candle holder following the star shape, or making a design of your own. These indentations will aid the baking process as moisture will escape through the holes.

● Transfer the candle holders to the microwave turntable plate. Because the shapes are quite thick, they will require a longer baking time. Bake on low for 30 minutes + 30 minutes + 20 minutes, medium low for 15 minutes + 15 minutes + 10 minutes, and medium for 5 minutes + 5 minutes. Remove the candle holders from the microwave oven and leave to cool before decorating. Using sandpaper, smooth off any rough edges or corners.

● Apply a coat of acrylic paint to both sides of each candle holder, choosing a dark color such as purple, dark red or blue. Then take a little gold metallic paint on your forefinger and lightly rub over the painted surface.

● When the paint is dry, squeeze a spot of quick-drying craft glue into each of the indentations in the surface of the dough and place a gold bead onto each of the glue spots. Leave the glue to dry. Apply three coats of satin varnish to both sides of each candle holder, leaving each coat to dry before applying the next.

● Place a small candle in the center of each star.

TEMPLATES AND CUTTERS

Bird-in-the-Bush

The charming little bird and tree motif in this candle sconce was inspired by Polish paper cuts popular in the nineteenth century. Use the sconce as a freestanding table ornament or hang it on the wall.

YOU WILL NEED

½ batch salt dough (see page 11)

Rolling pin

Flour

Pastry board

Tracing paper

Pencil

Scissors

Small knife

Modeling knife

Pointed modeling tool

Wooden skewer

Fine grade sandpaper

Acrylic spray paint

Newspaper

Acrylic paint in a darker color

Mixing palette

Small piece of synthetic sponge

Paintbrush

Satin polyurethane varnish

Epoxy resin adhesive

Two small metal right-angle
    brackets

Empty casing of a nightlight

Small candle

SAFETY NOTE
• Never leave burning
candles unattended.
Always place candles on a
heat-resistant surface and
do not let candles burn
down too low. Always
use spray paints in a
well-ventilated room.

● Roll out the dough to a thickness of ¼ inch on a lightly floured pastry board. Trace off the sconce and bottom templates on page 118. Cut out the template in paper and place on the rolled-out dough. Use a small knife to cut accurately around the bottom shape and roughly around the sconce. Using a smaller modeling knife, carefully cut around the bird and bush motif at the center of the sconce, removing the waste dough. Cut more accurately around the sconce shape and then using the modeling knife make tiny "V"-shaped cuts around the curved outside edge. Use a pointed modeling tool or a wooden skewer to make some decorative lines and features on the bird and the leaves of the bush.

● Roll a small ball of dough into a sausage about ⅜ inch in diameter. Cut it to fit around the outside edge of the bottom to act as a rim. Moisten the curved edge with water and then press the rolled sausage gently into place. Make rows of shallow indentations all over the surface of the bottom, using the blunt end of a wooden skewer. These indentations are not only decorative but will prevent the flat shape from rising and distorting during the baking process.

● Transfer the sconce and bottom to the microwave turntable plate and bake on low for 15 minutes + 15 minutes, medium low for 15 minutes, medium for 15 minutes, and medium high for 10 minutes. Remove from the microwave oven and leave to dry before decorating. Using sandpaper, smooth off any rough edges.

● Color the sconce and bottom on both sides, using an acrylic spray paint. Place the pieces on a sheet of newspaper to protect your work surface. Leave the paint to dry before applying the darker color. Spread a little of the darker paint onto a mixing palette and dip the sponge into the paint. Using a light dabbing motion, decorate the sconce and bottom with a subtle mottled pattern. Leave the paint to dry.

● Apply three coats of satin varnish to both sides of the sconce and bottom, leaving each coat to dry before applying the next.

● Attach the sconce back to the bottom, using strong epoxy resin adhesive. Hold the two pieces together in a right-angle position until the adhesive sets slightly. Use more of the epoxy resin adhesive to attach two small metal right-angle brackets to the join at the bottom of the sconce – the brackets will hold the join firm.

● Paint a nightlight casing to match the sconce and insert a small candle. Use strong epoxy resin adhesive to secure the casing in place on the bottom.

Tropical Fish Coat Hooks

A pair of brightly colored tropical fish to adorn plain metal coat hooks.
Why not make a shoal of little fish, one for each member of the family.

YOU WILL NEED

¼ batch salt dough (see page 11)

Rolling pin

Flour

Pastry board

Tracing paper

Pencil

Scissors

Small knife

Fine grade sandpaper

Paintbrushes

Acrylic paint

Satin polyurethane varnish

Metal coat hook

Epoxy resin adhesive

● Roll out the dough to a thickness of ¼ inch on a lightly floured pastry board. Trace off the fish template on page 119. Cut out the template twice and lay both on top of the rolled-out dough. Using the small knife, cut roughly around the outside. Then remove the waste dough and, using the point of the knife, cut into the smaller areas around the fins and tail. Roll two small balls of dough for the eyes. Moisten the eye area with a little water and press each eye into position.

● Transfer the fish to the microwave turntable plate and bake on low for 20 minutes, medium low for 10 minutes, and medium for 5 minutes + 5 minutes. Remove from the microwave oven and leave to cool. Using sandpaper, smooth off any rough areas.

● Apply a base coat of acrylic paint to both sides of the fish shapes and leave to dry. Paint on the colored features, using the photograph as a guide. When the paint has dried completely, apply three coats of satin varnish, leaving each coat to dry before applying the next.

● Screw the coat hook into position on the wall or on the back of a door. Attach the fish to the hook using epoxy resin adhesive (you could use double-sided adhesive pads instead of glue).

Stone Brooch

An elegant brooch made from the simplest of dough shapes bound together with fine silvery wire. The subtle mottled paint finish gives an almost stone-like appearance.

YOU WILL NEED

⅛ batch salt dough (see page 11)

Rolling pin

Flour

Pastry board

Tracing paper

Pencil

Scissors

Small knife

Wooden skewer

Fine grade sandpaper

Paintbrush

Acrylic paints

Newspaper

Mixing palette

Toothbrush

Satin polyurethane varnish

Fine silver wire

Wire cutter

Brooch clasp

Epoxy resin glue

● Roll out the dough to a thickness of ¼ inch on a lightly floured pastry board. Trace off the brooch templates on page 118. Cut out the templates and lay them on top of the rolled-out dough. Using a small knife, cut around the templates. Pierce a large hole at the center of each piece where indicated, using the blunt end of a wooden skewer.

● Transfer the pieces to the microwave turntable plate and bake on low for 10 minutes + 5 minutes, medium low for 5 minutes, and medium for 3 minutes. Remove the pieces from the microwave oven and leave to cool before painting. Using sandpaper, smooth off any rough edges.

● Apply two coats of acrylic paint to both sides of the brooch pieces (black and cream are effective color combinations). Leave the paint to dry.

● Lay the pieces face upward on a sheet of newspaper. Place a small amount of paint on a palette, add water, and mix to a watery consistency. Dip the bristles of an old toothbrush into the paint and aim the brush at the dough pieces, drawing the blade of a knife toward you across the bristles. This will cause a fine spray of paint to be deposited on the surface (see page 25). Choose colors that contrast with the first coat.

● When the paint is dry, apply three coats of satin varnish, leaving each coat to dry before applying the next. When the varnish is dry, place the disk on top of the triangle and bind the two together by passing the wire through the center hole and around the outside. Twist the ends of the wire on the reverse side to secure. Fix a brooch clasp to the reverse side, using epoxy resin glue.

Golden Baubles

*Decorating the tree is always the best part of the Christmas festivities. These
simple salt dough shapes have been sprayed with burnished gold paint and
have tiny bead droppers attached with colored threads.*

YOU WILL NEED

¼ batch salt dough (see page 11)
   will make 10 or 12 decorations
Rolling pin
Flour
Pastry board
Heart, star and triangular shaped
   cookie cutters (large size for
   the main shape and smaller
   canapé size for the cutouts)
Bodkin
Fine grade sandpaper
Sheet of newspaper
Acrylic metallic finish spray paint
Paintbrush
Satin polyurethane varnish
Sewing needle
Colored sewing thread
Small beads

● Roll out the dough to a thickness of ¼ inch on a lightly floured pastry board.
Using the cookie cutters, stamp out heart, star and triangular shapes. Then
using the smaller canapé cutters, stamp out a motif from the center of each one.
Using a bodkin, pierce a hole for the hanging loop at the top of each decoration
and also some holes to hang the beads from.

● Transfer half the decorations at a time to the microwave turntable plate and
bake on low for 15 minutes + 15 minutes, medium low for 10 minutes +
10 minutes, and medium for 5 minutes + 5 minutes. Remove them from the
microwave oven and leave to cool. Using sandpaper, smooth off any
rough edges.

● Place the decorations on a large sheet of newspaper and spray the metallic
paint on both sides, leaving the paint to dry before turning the shape over.

● Apply three coats of satin varnish to both sides, leaving each coat to dry
before applying the next.

● Using colored sewing thread, hang some
small beads from the pierced holes. Pass
four 8-inch lengths of thread through the
hole at the top of each shape and tie the
ends together to form a hanging loop.

> **SAFETY NOTE**
> ● Always use spray paints
> in a well-ventilated room.

Sunburst Clock

*Now you really can tell the time by looking at the sun! This fiery sunburst
clock has been given an effective antiqued look simply by using a crackle
varnish over gold metallic paint.*

YOU WILL NEED

1 batch salt dough (see page 11)

Rolling pin

Flour

Pastry board

Tracing paper

Pencil

Scissors

Small knife

Alphabet cookie cutters

Fine grade sandpaper

Sheet of newspaper

Gold metallic acrylic spray paint

Paintbrush

Satin polyurethane varnish

Crackle varnish kit

Burnt umber oil paint

Soft cloth

Epoxy resin glue

Bradawl or hand drill

Clock mechanism and a pair of
  clock hands

TIP
When painting and
varnishing the numerals, it
is a good idea to place a
strip of double-sided
adhesive tape to a piece of
card, peel off the backing
paper, and press the
numerals onto the sticky
surface. This holds them in
position and keeps your
hands clean.

● Roll out the dough to a thickness of ¼ inch on a lightly floured pastry board. Trace off the sun template on page 119. Cut out the template and place on top of the rolled-out dough. Carefully cut around the outside of the template, using a small knife. Remove the paper template and pinch each of the points slightly between your thumb and forefinger. Gather up the offcuts of dough and reroll to the same thickness. Using the "I," "X," and "V" cutters, make Roman numerals from I to XII.

● Transfer the sunburst shape and the Roman numerals to the microwave turntable plate and bake on low for 30 minutes + 30 minutes, medium low for 15 minutes + 15 minutes, and medium for 5 minutes + 5 minutes. Remove them from the microwave oven and leave to cool before painting. Using sandpaper, smooth off any rough edges.

● Place the clock shape on a sheet of newspaper and spray on two coats of gold metallic paint to both sides of the clock and the numerals. Leave the paint to dry.

● Apply three coats of satin varnish to the reverse side of the clock and to both sides of the numerals, leaving each coat to dry before applying the next.

● When the satin varnish is dry, turn the clock over and apply the first step of the crackle varnish. Leave to dry for 30 minutes then apply the second step. When the second coat is dry and the surface is well crackled, rub a little burnt umber oil paint into the cracks, using a soft cloth (see page 25).

● Attach the numerals in position, using epoxy resin glue. When the glue has dried and the numerals are firmly in position, use a bradawl or hand drill to pierce a hole at the center of the clock ready to receive the clock spindle. Fit the clock mechanism and hands following the manufacturer's directions.

NOTE
● The numerals will be
ready before the main
piece, so remove when
they are dry.

2
MOLDING

Fancy Egg Cups

Decorative egg cups to add a touch of color to the breakfast table. Original and fun, yet very simple to make using empty eggshells as molds. At Easter time, use them to display colorful dyed or painted eggs.

YOU WILL NEED

¼ batch salt dough (see page 11)

Rolling pin

Flour

Pastry board

Large star-shaped cookie cutter

Empty eggshells

Paintbrushes

Acrylic paints

Satin polyurethane varnish

● Roll out the dough to a thickness of ¼ inch on a lightly floured pastry board. Cut out large star shapes, using a cookie cutter. Place the cutout shapes over the empty eggshells and gently smooth the points down the side of the shell (see page 15).

● Place the dough-covered eggshells on the pastry board. Gather up the waste dough and roll into sausage shapes about ⅜ inch in diameter. Use the sausage shapes to form two rings for each egg cup to act as a stand. The smaller ring has a diameter of 1⅛ inches and the larger one 1¼ inches. Moisten the surface of the rings and the underside of the egg cup with water. Place the smaller ring on the larger one and then place the egg cup on top.

● Transfer them to the microwave turntable plate. (As the egg cups are quite small, you can bake three or four at a time.) Bake on low for 10 minutes + 10 minutes, medium low for 5 minutes + 5 minutes, and medium for 2 minutes + 2 minutes. When the dough is dry, remove from the microwave oven and leave to cool. Do not remove the egg mold while the dough is still warm as this may cause damage. Using sandpaper, smooth off any rough edges.

● Apply two coats of acrylic paint to the egg cups. Color each ring and its cup a different shade.

● When the paint is dry, apply three coats of satin varnish, leaving each coat to dry before applying the next.

Coil Vase

Salt dough vases make perfect containers for dried flower arrangements.
Fascinating, convoluted textures can be achieved by coiling rolls of raw salt
dough around a card mold. The uneven surface is farther enhanced by using
contrast colors over the bottom coat.

YOU WILL NEED

½ batch salt dough (see page 11)
Tracing paper
Pencil
Scissors
Thin card
Double-sided adhesive tape
Masking tape
Plastic food wrap
Rolling pin
Flour
Pastry board
Small knife
Modeling tools
Newspaper
Acrylic spray paint
Acrylic paint
Flat mixing palette
Small synthetic sponge
Paintbrush
Satin polyurethane varnish

● Trace off the card mold templates on page 121 and cut out the shapes in thin card. Bend the side piece to form a slightly tapered tube and join the side seam together with double-sided adhesive tape. Attach the round bottom to the mold, using tabs of masking tape (see Making and using card molds, page 16). Cover the card mold with a layer of plastic food wrap to prevent the dough from sticking.

● Roll out a small ball of dough to a thickness of ¼ inch on a lightly floured pastry board. Use the original tracing of the bottom to cut out a small dough round. Invert the card mold and place the dough round over the bottom, pressing gently into position. Divide the remaining dough into balls and roll each one into a sausage shape about ½ inch in diameter. Coil the rolls around the mold beginning at the bottom, joining on new rolls of dough as you go. Continue coiling until you reach the edge of the mold (see Coiling around a mold, page 17).

● Using a moistened modeling tool, smooth out the joins between the coils (this will insure that they do not come apart during baking as well as making an interesting texture).

● Transfer the coiled mold to the microwave turntable plate and bake on low for 30 minutes + 30 minutes, medium low for 20 minutes + 20 minutes, and medium for 10 minutes + 5 minutes. Remove the mold from the microwave oven and leave to cool on the mold. Do not attempt to remove the mold while the dough is still warm, as this may result in warping and damage. Remove the card mold when the dough is completely cool.

● Place the dry dough vase on a large sheet of newspaper and use acrylic spray paint to color the inside and the outside. Apply two coats if the coverage is not dense enough. Leave to dry. Spread a small amount of a contrasting color paint onto a flat palette. Dip a small synthetic sponge into the paint and lightly wipe over the convoluted surface of the vase. The colored paint will be deposited on the raised parts of the coiling, accentuating the irregular pattern and creating an interesting effect.

● After the decorative paintwork has dried completely, apply three coats of satin varnish, leaving each coat to dry before applying the next.

Party Bowls

*Molded around simple card shapes, these conical bowls work well as containers
for party snacks. Decorate in this bold primitive style or choose your own
design, perhaps to match the pattern or color scheme of your favorite
china or linen.*

YOU WILL NEED

1 batch salt dough (see page 11),
    makes two bowls
Rolling pin
Flour
Pastry board
Tracing paper
Pencil
Scissors
Thin card
Double-sided adhesive tape
Masking tape
Plastic food wrap
Small knife
Modeling knife
Craft knife
Paintbrushes
Acrylic paints in two colors
Satin polyurethane varnish

● Divide the dough in half and roll out each portion to a thickness of ¼ inch
on a lightly floured pastry board. Trace off the templates for the card mold on
page 120. Cut out the relevant pieces in thin card. Bend the main part of the
mold to form a tapered shape. Join the side using double-sided adhesive tape
and attach the bottom piece using tabs of masking tape (see Making and using
card molds, page 16). Cover the mold with a layer of plastic food wrap to
prevent the dough from sticking.

● Place the tracing of the side piece on the rolled-out dough and cut around it
with a small knife, leaving a margin of about ¾ inch along the bottom edge.
Remove the excess dough. Carefully lift the cut dough shape and wrap it
around the mold (see Making and using card molds, page 16). Press the excess
dough together across the bottom of the mold and then press the edges along
the join at the side. Smooth out the joins with a moistened modeling knife or
your fingers. Trim the edge level and then smooth the cut edge with the blade of
a craft knife, or your fingers.

● Transfer the dough-covered mold to the microwave turntable plate and bake
on low for 20 minutes + 20 minutes, medium low for 15 minutes + 15 minutes,
and medium for 10 minutes + 10 minutes + 5 minutes. Remove the mold from
the microwave oven and leave to cool, still supported by the card mold. Do not
attempt to remove the mold while the dough is still warm as this may cause the
shape to warp. Bake the second bowl in the same way. Remove the card mold
and using sandpaper, smooth off any rough edges.

● Apply two coats of acrylic paint to the outside and inside of each bowl.
Paint the inside a different color from the outside. Leave the paint to dry
and then, using a paintbrush, add decorative details such as bold stripes or
zigzags and a stripe around the rim.

● After the decorative paintwork has
dried completely, apply three
coats of satin varnish,
leaving each coat to
dry before applying
the next.

Spiral Wire Trinket Holders

Small cone-shaped holders for keeping pencils or trinkets tidy, each is supported with an elegant twisted spiral of wire and has a decorative silver paint finish.

YOU WILL NEED

¼ batch salt dough (see page 11)
    makes two or three cones
Rolling pin
Flour
Pastry board
Tracing paper
Pencil
Thin card
Scissors
Double-sided adhesive tape
Plastic food wrap
Small knife
Modeling tool
Fine grade sandpaper
Paintbrushes
Acrylic paints
Silver metallic acrylic paint
Flat mixing palette
Small synthetic sponge
Satin polyurethane varnish
Wire cutter
Wire coat hanger
Pliers

● Roll out the dough to a thickness of ¼ inch on a lightly floured pastry board. Trace off the template on page 120. Cut out as many as you need from thin card. Bend the card to form a cone shape and secure in place, using double-sided adhesive tape (see Making and using card molds, page 16). Cover the card mold with plastic food wrap to prevent the dough from sticking.

● Place the original tracing on the rolled-out dough and cut around it. Carefully lift the dough shape and wrap it around the card mold, gently pressing the edges together along the join. Smooth out the join with a moistened modeling tool or your fingers. Trim the edge level and smooth out the cut edge.

● Transfer the dough-covered mold to the microwave turntable plate. Bake on low for 15 minutes + 15 minutes, medium low for 10 minutes + 10 minutes, and medium for 3 minutes + 3 minutes. When the dough shapes are dry, remove from the microwave oven and leave to cool, still supported by the card molds. When the dough cones are cool, remove the card molds. Using sandpaper, smooth off any surface unevenness.

● Apply two coats of acrylic paint to the cone shapes and leave to dry. Sponge a little silver metallic paint onto the painted surface of the cone. When dry, apply three coats of satin varnish, leaving each coat to dry before applying the next.

● Cut a 28-inch length of wire from a coat hanger and bend it in half. Using pliers, bend the wire to form a spiral stand to support the cone.

Greek Vase

*This grand, urn-style vase with two elegantly curving handles is designed to
hold a smaller glass vase or container. Fill the glass container with water so
you are able to display fresh flowers of the season without damaging
the salt dough.*

YOU WILL NEED

1 batch salt dough (see page 11)

Rolling pin

Flour

Pastry board

Tracing paper

Pencil

Thin card

Scissors

Double-sided adhesive tape

Masking tape

Plastic food wrap

Small knife

Epoxy resin adhesive

Paintbrushes

Acrylic paints

Flat mixing palette

Small synthetic sponge

Satin polyurethane varnish

● Roll out the dough to a thickness of ¼ inch on a lightly floured pastry board. Trace off the tall vase template on page 121. Cut out the side and bottom in thin card. Bend the side to form a tapered tube and secure with double-sided adhesive tape. Attach the circular bottom with tabs of masking tape (see Making and using card molds, page 16). Cover the card mold with a layer of plastic food wrap to prevent the dough from sticking.

● Place the original tracings on the rolled-out dough and cut around them with a small knife. Wrap the side shape around the card mold, pressing the straight edges together. Then place the circular bottom piece into position and press the edges together firmly. Trim the edge level with a small knife. Smooth out the joins and the cut edge with your fingers or a modeling tool moistened with water (see Making and using card molds, page 16).

● Gather up some of the waste dough and roll into two 8-inch long sausage shapes about ¾ inch in diameter and tapering at both ends. Model each to form a "comma" shape (these will be baked separately and glued onto the vase afterwards to form the handles).

● Transfer the dough-covered mold and the handles to the microwave turntable plate. Make sure that the mold stands upside down, otherwise the dough will sag during the baking process. Bake on low for 30 minutes + 30 minutes, medium low for 20 minutes + 20 minutes, and medium for 10 minutes + 10 minutes + 5 minutes. Remove from the microwave oven and leave to cool. Do not remove the mold while the dough is still warm as this may cause damage and warping. Using sandpaper, smooth off any rough edges when the dough is completely cool.

● Fix the handles in position on either side of the vase, using a strong epoxy resin adhesive. Leave the adhesive to set hard.

● Apply two coats of acrylic paint in a pale color to act as a bottom coat and a sealant. Take two contrasting colored paints and spread a little of each onto a flat mixing palette. Use a small synthetic sponge to smear each color lightly over the bottom coat. This creates a delicate mottled effect.

● When the decorative paintwork is completely dry, apply three coats of satin varnish, leaving each coat to dry before applying the next.

Leaf Plates

*Delicate leaves make excellent templates for stencils. Paint these gently
curving plates in a color resembling terracotta, then add the surface decoration
using pretty pastel shades around stencils.*

● Divide the dough into three equal portions. Roll out one portion to a thickness of ¼ inch on a lightly floured pastry board. Cover the concave surface of the plate with a layer of plastic food wrap to prevent the dough from sticking to it. Carefully lift the dough from the pastry board, supporting it underneath with your hand. Lay the dough on top of the plate and press gently with your fingers so it molds to the concave shape. Using a small sharp knife, cut away the excess dough close to the edge of the plate. Then, using the blade of a modeling knife, gently tap the cut edge to smooth away any irregularities.

● Transfer the dough-covered plate to the microwave turntable plate and bake on low for 20 minutes + 20 minutes, medium low for 20 minutes, and medium for 10 minutes + 5 minutes. Remove from the microwave oven and leave to cool. Do not attempt to remove the dough plate from the mold while it is still warm as this may cause warping.

● When the dough has cooled completely, carefully prize it away from the mold using a small knife. Using sandpaper, smooth off any rough edges. At this stage you can repair any small cracks with some fresh dough, returning the plate to the microwave oven to dry out again. Make two more plates in the same way.

● Apply two coats of acrylic paint in a terracotta color to both sides of the dough plates as bottom coat and sealant and leave to dry. Invert one plate and place it on a sheet of plain paper. Trace around the outside with a pencil and cut out the paper round with scissors. Cut another round about ½ inch in from the outside edge. Attach the resulting ring of paper around the outside of the plate with masking tape tabs (this will mask off a border area ready for decoration). Place a small nicely shaped leaf in the center of the plate. Mix some pastel colored acrylic paints on a flat palette. Sponge the paint onto the surface of the plate around the leaf. Remove the leaf and the paper ring when the paint has dried to reveal the negative image beneath. Using a small brush, paint decorative dashes around the outer border. Decorate the other two plates in the same way, using differently shaped leaves and toning pastel colors.

● When all the decorative paintwork is dry, apply three coats of satin varnish to both sides of the dough plates, leaving each coat to dry thoroughly before applying the next.

Ruby Red Conical Box

*A most unusually shaped box with a coiled lid and three curled legs, in which
to hide your treasures, richly decorated with deep reds and a hint of gold.*

YOU WILL NEED

½ batch salt dough (see page 11)
Rolling pin
Flour
Pastry board
Tracing paper
Pencil
Scissors
Thin card
Double-sided adhesive tape
Plastic food wrap
Small knife
Modeling tool
Fine grade sandpaper
Epoxy resin adhesive
Paintbrushes
Acrylic paint
Small sponge
Gold metallic acrylic paint
Satin polyurethane varnish

● Roll out the dough to a thickness of ¼ inch on a lightly floured pastry board. Trace off the conical template on page 121. Cut out the shape in thin card. Bend the card to form the cone shape and secure with double-sided adhesive tape. Cover the card mold with plastic food wrap to prevent the dough from sticking.

● Place the original tracing on the rolled-out dough and cut around it with a small knife. Wrap the dough around the conical mold and press the edges together. Smooth out the join with your fingers or a modeling tool moistened with water. Trim the upper edge level and smooth out the cut edge with your fingers or the blade of a modeling knife.

● Gather up the waste dough and roll into a sausage about ½ inch in diameter. Coil up the sausage to form a circle to fit the upper edge of the box (this will be the lid). Break off a small piece of dough and roll it into a small ball. Press it to the center of the lid. Roll the remaining dough into three sausages about 6 inches long and coil each to form "S" shapes (these will act as legs for the box).

● Transfer the box, lid and legs to the microwave turntable plate and bake on low for 30 minutes + 30 minutes, medium low for 20 minutes + 20 minutes, and medium for 10 minutes + 10 minutes + 10 minutes. Remove from the microwave oven and leave to cool. Do not remove the card mold while the dough is warm as this may cause damage and warping.

● Use strong epoxy resin glue to fix the three legs in place around the bottom of the conical box. Leave the glue to set.

● Apply two coats of acrylic paint to the box and lid and leave to dry. Sponge on some gold metallic paint lightly over the painted surface. When the decorative paintwork has dried, apply three coats of satin varnish, leaving each coat to dry before applying the next.

Fishy Dishes

*These dishes make delightful wall decorations — each fish seems to have its
own individual personality and facial expression. The use of simple templates
and basic molding methods again produce effective results, and the shallow
concave shape offers a large area for creative decoration.*

YOU WILL NEED

½ batch salt dough (see page 11)
    makes two dishes

Rolling pin

Flour

Pastry board

Tracing paper

Pencil

Scissors

Plain paper

Small knife

Two small saucers about 5 inches
    in diameter to use as molds

Plastic food wrap

Fine grade sandpaper

Paintbrushes

Acrylic paints

Satin polyurethane varnish

● Roll out the dough to a thickness of ¼ inch on a lightly floured pastry board. Trace off the fish template on page 122 and cut out as many shapes as you require in plain paper. Place the templates on the rolled-out dough and cut around the outside edge carefully using a small knife.

● Invert the saucers and place them on your counter. Cover the convex side with a layer of plastic wrap to prevent the dough from sticking. Remove the turntable plate from the microwave oven and place one saucer in the center. Carefully lift up one dough fish shape and place it over the inverted saucer mold. Smooth the dough with your fingers so it fits the convex shape. The template allows for a narrow rim around the outside of the saucer (this is indicated with a dotted line).

● Return the dough-covered mold on the turntable plate back to the microwave oven and bake on low for 20 minutes + 20 minutes, medium low for 20 minutes, and medium for 10 minutes + 5 minutes. Remove the dish from the microwave oven and leave to cool. Do not remove the saucer mold while the dough is warm as this may cause warping and damage.

● Prize the dish away from the mold, using a small knife, when it is completely cool. Using sandpaper, smooth off any rough edges.

● Apply two coats of white acrylic paint as a sealant and bottom coat to both sides of the dish. Leave to dry. Paint on details and features, using the photograph as a guide, or you could create your own designs.

● Apply three coats of satin varnish when the decorative paintwork is dry, leaving each coat to dry before applying the next.

Fruits of the Forest Dishes

*Fresh leaves gathered from the garden are used to emboss the intricate network
of veins onto the surface of these realistic leafy dishes.*

YOU WILL NEED

¼ batch salt dough (see page 11)
    makes two
Rolling pin
Flour
Pastry board
Leaf-shaped dishes as molds
Plastic food wrap
Small knife
Modeling tool
Large fresh leaves
Paintbrushes
Acrylic paints
Flat mixing palette
Small sponge
Satin polyurethane varnish

● Roll out the dough to a thickness of ¼ inch on a lightly floured pastry board. Cover the inside of the leaf dish molds with plastic food wrap to prevent the dough from sticking (the molds for the dishes shown here were made from wood). Cut a piece of dough approximately the same size as the dish and press it into place so that the dough fits the concave shape. Use a small knife to trim around the edge, following the curved edge of the mold. Smooth out the cut edge with your finger or the end of a moistened modeling tool.

● Press the leaf firmly onto the surface of the dough. The veins on the underside will leave an impression (see Embossed decoration, page 20).

● Transfer the dishes to the microwave turntable plate and bake on low for 15 minutes + 15 minutes, medium low for 10 minutes + 10 minutes, and medium for 5 minutes + 3 minutes. Remove the dishes from the microwave oven and leave to cool. Do not remove the mold while the dough is still warm as this may cause damage and warping. When the dough is completely dry, remove it from the mold using a small knife.

● Apply a coat of light cream paint to both sides of the dishes and leave to dry. Then sponge on a darker color, lightly on the upper side to accentuate the embossed pattern and more densely on the underside and around the edge.

● When the decorative paint has dried, apply three coats of satin varnish, leaving each coat to dry before applying the next.

Exotic Fruit Bowls

*Bright orange and turquoise blue patterns lend these unusually shaped fruit
bowls a slightly tropical flavor. Made by first cutting simple square and
triangular shapes from rolled-out dough and then molding over glass bowls of
different sizes. Add a circular bottom to each to give character and stability.*

YOU WILL NEED

1 batch salt dough (see page 11)
  makes one large bowl and two
  smaller ones
Rolling pin
Flour
Pastry board
Pastry brush
Plain paper
Pencil
Ruler
Scissors
Small sharp knife
Selection of round glass bowls
  in different sizes,
  one approximately
  2½-quart capacity and
  two 1-pint capacity
Modeling tools
Fine grade sandpaper
Paintbrushes
Acrylic paints
Satin polyurethane varnish

● Divide the dough in half and then divide one half into two. Roll out each portion in turn to a thickness of ¼ inch on a lightly floured pastry board. On a plain sheet of paper draw out the square and triangular templates required for cutting the dough shapes: a 9-inch square for the large bowl and a 5-inch square and a 6-inch equilateral triangle for the small bowls. Cut out the paper shapes and lay each in turn on to a rolled-out dough piece. Carefully cut around the outside of the paper template with a small sharp knife. Remove the excess dough.

● Invert the glass bowls and lay them flat on your counter. Cover the outsides with a layer of plastic food wrap. Carefully lift each dough shape, supporting it underneath with your hand, and place it over the appropriate mold. Try to center the dough pieces and gently smooth the corners flat down the side of the molds.

● Then add a round bottom to each of the bowls. Roll a small ball of dough into a sausage about ⅝ inch in diameter and long enough to form a round at the bottom. Using a small knife, cut the ends of the sausage diagonally. Moisten the bottom area of each bowl and the cut ends of the sausage with a little water. Gently press the bottom into position, making sure that the ends are secure. Smooth out the joins, using a slightly moistened modeling tool (see Adding a bottom to a bowl, page 19).

● Transfer each dough-covered mold, one at a time, to the microwave turntable plate and bake the large bowl on low for 30 minutes + 30 minutes, medium low for 20 minutes + 20 minutes, and medium for 10 minutes + 5 minutes + 5 minutes; and the small square and triangular bowls on low for 20 minutes + 20 minutes, medium low for 10 minutes + 10 minutes, and medium for 10 minutes + 5 minutes. Remove them from the microwave oven and leave to cool, still supported by the mold. Do not remove the mold while the dough is still warm as this will cause warping. When completely dry carefully prize the dough bowls away from the molds using a knife. Using sandpaper, smooth off any rough edges.

● Apply two coats of a light or neutral color acrylic paint to act as a sealant and a bottom coat for the painted decoration. Using bright oranges and turquoise blues, paint bold swirls and spirals freehand on both the inside and outside surfaces.

● When the paintwork has dried completely, apply three coats of satin varnish inside and outside each bowl, leaving each coat to dry before applying the next.

Ribbon Dishes

The natural-looking free shape of these potpourri dishes is created simply by letting the molded dough form its own shape around the glass or ceramic mold and leaving the edge untrimmed. Delicate paint effects using a natural sponge complement the softly curving form.

YOU WILL NEED

1 batch salt dough (see page 11) makes two bowls

Rolling pin

Flour

Pastry board

2½-quart capacity glass bowl and a 2-pint capacity bowl to use as molds

Plastic food wrap

Modeling knife

Small knife

Paintbrushes

Acrylic paints

Flat mixing palette

Small natural sponge

Satin polyurethane varnish

Two colored ribbons

● Use two-thirds of the dough for the larger bowl and the remaining one-third for the smaller one. Roll out the dough pieces to a thickness of ¼ inch on a lightly floured pastry board. Try to keep the pieces round or oval-shaped. Invert the glass bowls and place them on your counter. Cover the convex side with a layer of plastic food wrap to prevent the dough from sticking to the mold.

● Carefully lift up the rolled-out dough shapes and place on the relevant mold. Try to position the dough centrally. Gently press the edges of the dough so they lie smoothly around the sides of the molds. Do not trim at this stage – just round off the wavy edge smoothly with your fingers or a moistened modeling tool. Cut eight small, irregularly-shaped holes about an inch from the rim of each dish, at least 1½ inches away from each other, to thread ribbon through when the dishes are finished.

● Transfer each bowl separately to the microwave turntable plate and bake the large bowl on low for 30 minutes + 30 minutes, medium low for 20 minutes + 20 minutes, and medium for 10 minutes + 5 minutes + 5 minutes; and the small bowl on low for 20 minutes + 20 minutes, medium low for 10 minutes + 10 minutes, and medium for 10 minutes + 5 minutes. Remove them from the microwave oven and leave to cool on the molds. Do not attempt to remove the dishes from the molds while the dough is still warm as this may result in warping and damage. Carefully prize the dry dishes away from the molds, using a small knife.

● Apply two coats of acrylic paint in a light or neutral color to both sides of the dough shapes as a sealant and bottom coat. When the paint is dry, spread a little paint in a contrasting color onto a flat mixing palette. Dip the small natural sponge into the paint and press the sponge against the painted surface of the bowls. The irregular holes in the sponge will create a pleasing mottled effect. Decorate the inside and the outside of both bowls in this way.

● When the decorative paintwork has dried completely, apply three coats of satin varnish, leaving each coat to dry before applying the next.

● When the varnish is dry, thread ribbon through the holes around the rim of the bowl and finish by tying the ends together in a bow.

Embossed Wall Tiles

With a little imagination you can find any number of three-dimensional objects to be used successfully as embossing tools, from keys and wooden clothes pegs to natural forms such as sea shells and leaves. A collection of simple embossed salt dough tiles makes delightful wall decorations.

YOU WILL NEED

½ batch salt dough (see page 11) makes four tiles

Rolling pin

Flour

Pastry board

Small knife

Assorted objects for embossing such as keys, wooden clothes pegs and shells

Wooden skewer

Paintbrushes

Acrylic paints

Small synthetic sponge

Satin polyurethane varnish

● Roll out the dough to a thickness of ¼ inch on a lightly floured pastry board. Cut out four 4¾-inch squares, using a small knife. You could make a paper template of a square. Create the embossed patterns by pressing the keys, clothes pegs or shells firmly into the surface of the dough. Take care not to press right through to the other side. Use a wooden skewer to emboss a border groove about ¼ inch in from the cut edge around all four sides and then use the end of the skewer to create the decorative dashes. These indentations and embossed patterns are not only decorative but aid the drying process and help to keep the dough shape flat during baking.

● Transfer the tiles to the microwave turntable plate and bake on low for 30 minutes + 30 minutes, medium low for 20 minutes + 20 minutes, and medium for 10 minutes + 10 minutes + 5 minutes. Remove the tiles from the microwave oven and leave to cool.

● Apply two coats of white acrylic paint to act as a sealant and bottom coat. Then take two other colors and spread a little of each onto a flat mixing palette. Using a synthetic sponge, smear the paint lightly over the bottom coat to accentuate the embossed patterns. Make the border a different color.

● When the decorative paint has dried completely, apply two coats of satin varnish, leaving each coat to dry before applying the next.

Embossed Trinket Box

Keep your jewelry and trinkets safe inside this pretty little lidded box. Molded around a square glass bottle, the flat sides provide an excellent surface for the embossed spiral decoration. Add a feminine touch by coloring first in a rosy pink, then adding a blush of lilac.

YOU WILL NEED

¼ batch salt dough (see page 11)

Rolling pin

Flour

Pastry board

Small square glass bottle (about 2½ inches square) as a mold

Plain paper

Pencil

Scissors

Small knife

Plastic food wrap

Modeling tool

Wire coat hanger

Wire cutter

Fine grade sandpaper

Paintbrushes

Acrylic paints

Satin polyurethane varnish

● Roll out the dough to a thickness of ¼ inch on a lightly floured pastry board. Stand the glass bottle on a piece of plain paper. Trace around the bottom with a pencil and cut out the shape twice. Lay the paper templates on the rolled-out dough and cut around the edges, using a small sharp knife. Use one dough square as the bottom and the other as a lid.

● From the remaining dough cut a 2½-inch wide strip, long enough to fit around the circumference of the bottle. Cover the bottle with a layer of plastic food wrap to prevent the dough from sticking. Turn the bottle upside down and wrap the dough strip around the sides near the bottom. Press the short edges together to make a neat join. Place the square bottom onto the bottle mold and press the edges together. Smooth out the joins with a modeling tool moistened with water.

● Cut a 6-inch length of wire from a coat hanger, using a wire cutter. Bend the wire into a spiral shape, leaving a "tail" at the center to use as a handle. Press the wire shape firmly onto the raw dough on each side of the box (see Embossed decoration, page 20).

● Take five small pieces of dough and roll each into a small ball. Use one as a knob for the lid and four as feet for the box. Moisten the center of the lid and the four corners of the underside with water and press the dough balls gently into place. Transfer the dough lid and the bottle mold to the microwave turntable plate. (You may need to support the bottle by standing it upside down in a mug or small dish to prevent it falling over as the plate revolves.) Bake on low for 20 minutes + 20 minutes, medium low for 10 minutes + 10 minutes, and medium for 5 minutes + 5 minutes. Remove from the microwave oven and leave to cool before removing from the mold.

● Slide the box from the bottle mold when it is completely cool. Using sandpaper smooth off any roughness.

● Apply two coats of acrylic paint to the box and lid as a base color and sealant. Take a small amount of a contrasting color paint on the end of your finger and rub over the painted surface to accentuate the embossed pattern. When the decorative paintwork is dry, apply three coats of polyurethane varnish, leaving each coat to dry before applying the next.

Burnished Bowls

Bowls and containers molded from salt dough are an excellent vehicle for all types of surface decoration. Many pleasing and attractive results can be achieved by using relief patterns made from dough applied in the raw state. The spiral pattern shown here was made from a simple cutout shape while the finer design was drawn on using a modeling syringe.

YOU WILL NEED

1 batch salt dough (see page 11)
    makes two bowls
Rolling pin
Flour
Pastry board
Shallow ceramic bowls as molds
    about 8–10 inches in diameter
Plastic food wrap
Small knife
Modeling knife
Modeling tool or toothpick
Modeling syringe
Fine grade sandpaper
Paintbrushes
Acrylic paints
Flat mixing palette
Small synthetic sponge
Gold metallic finish acrylic paint
Satin polyurethane varnish

● Divide the dough into equal portions. Roll out each to a thickness of ¼ inch on a lightly floured pastry board. Invert the molds and cover the convex side with a layer of plastic food wrap to prevent the dough from sticking. Carefully lift up the pieces of rolled-out dough and place each on a mold, gently pressing the dough flat around the shape. Trim the edge level, using a small knife. Smooth the cut edge using your finger or a modeling tool moistened with water. Mold two bowls in this way.

● To make the relief decoration, gather up the waste dough and reroll to a thickness of ¼ inch. Cut a small round of dough using a modeling knife and then cut each into a spiral shape. Moisten the surface of the molded bowl with water and press the spiral shape into position. Smooth out the joins with a modeling tool moistened with water and then using a pointed modeling tool or a toothpick make decorative indentations around the spirals; this will help keep the decoration in place and also aid the drying process (see Adding surface textures, page 19). For the finer string-like decoration, place a small ball of dough inside a modeling syringe, insert the plunger, and gently squeeze to extrude a thin line of dough. "Draw" a pattern directly onto the moistened surface of the molded bowl.

● Transfer the dough-covered molds, one at a time, to the microwave turntable plate and bake on low for 30 minutes + 30 minutes, medium low for 20 minutes + 20 minutes, and medium for 10 minutes + 10 minutes + 5 minutes. Remove the molds from the microwave oven and leave to dry. Do not remove the mold while the dough is still warm as this may cause damage and warping. When completely dry, prize the dough bowl from the mold with a small knife. Using sandpaper, smooth off any rough edges when the dough is completely cool.

● Apply two coats of acrylic paint to each of the bowls as a sealant and bottom color. Then spread two toning colors on a mixing palette and using a small synthetic sponge, smear the two colors randomly over the painted surface. When the paint has dried, apply gold metallic paint in the same way, to highlight the relief decoration and create an interesting mottled effect inside the bowls. Leave the decorative paintwork to dry thoroughly.

● Apply three coats of satin varnish, leaving each coat to dry before applying the next.

Two-Piece African Bowl and Vase

These earthy, African-inspired bowls are unusual in that the shape tapers inward toward the top. If a mold of this shape were used, it would be impossible to remove it without destroying the dough shape. Therefore these particular bowls have to be made in two pieces and joined to form the complete shape.

YOU WILL NEED

1 batch salt dough (see page 11) makes two

Rolling pin

Flour

Pastry board

Small ceramic bowls to use as molds (about 5 inches in diameter)

Straight-sided terracotta flower pot

Plastic food wrap

Small knife

Modeling knife

Fine grade sandpaper

Paintbrushes

Acrylic paints

Flat mixing palette

Small synthetic sponges

Scissors

Satin polyurethane varnish

● Divide the dough into quarters and roll out each portion to a thickness of ¼ inch on a lightly floured pastry board. Cover the convex side of the ceramic bowl with plastic food wrap to prevent the dough from sticking. Lift a piece of rolled dough and place it on the mold, pressing the dough with your fingers so it lies flat. Trim the edge level using a small knife.

● Transfer the dough-covered mold to the microwave turntable plate and bake on low for 20 minutes + 20 minutes, and medium low for 15 minutes + 15 minutes. When the dough is almost dry, remove from the microwave oven and leave to cool. Do not remove the mold while the dough is still warm as this may cause damage and warping. Prize the dough shape carefully from the mold with a small knife when it is completely cool and keep to one side. This will form the bottom of the bowl.

● Repeat the molding process with another piece of dough but this time cut a circle around the bottom (this will form the upper part of the bowl). Roll a small ball of waste dough into a sausage about ½ inch in diameter and long enough to fit around the opening. This will form the rim. Trim the ends of the sausage at right angles to make a neat join. Moisten the edge of the opening with a little water and gently press the rim into position, pressing the trimmed ends together. Using a moistened modeling tool, smooth out the joins. Bake the upper part as before and remove from the mold.

● Place the two parts of the bowl together and press small balls of raw dough to cover the join, inside and outside. Using a modeling tool moistened with water, smooth out the join. Return the bowl to the microwave oven to dry the fresh dough join, baking on low for 30 minutes, medium low for 20 minutes, and medium for 20 minutes. When dry, remove from the oven and leave to cool. Using sandpaper, smooth off any roughness around the joined area.

● Apply two coats of acrylic paint in a terracotta color as a sealant and bottom coat. Then paint the upper part and the rim black. Using a small sponge and cream-colored acrylic paint, make a mottled pattern over the darker upper area. Cut another piece of sponge into a "V" or triangular shape. Dip it into the paint and use it to make the other bold patterns running around the side of the bowl.

● When the paintwork has dried, apply three coats of satin varnish inside and outside, leaving each coat to dry before applying the next.

VASE
● Repeat the process described for the bowl, but mold the bottom half over a straight-sided terracotta flower pot.

3
MODELING

Daisy Pictures

Fresh as a daisy! These three-dimensional flower pictures make a pretty pair when hung together on a wall. The natural hessian backing gives a pleasing country look.

YOU WILL NEED

¼ batch salt dough (see page 11)
    makes two
Rolling pin
Flour
Pastry board
Large petal-shaped cutters
Small round canapé cutter
Toothpick
Garlic press
Paintbrushes
Acrylic paints
Satin polyurethane varnish
Short lengths of narrow
    wooden edging
Two 4-inch squares of plywood
Wood glue
Molding pins
Hammer
Hessian fabric
Double-sided tape
Two blocks of wood about
    ¾ inch square x ½ inch deep
Epoxy resin adhesive

● Roll out the dough to a thickness of ⅛ inch on a lightly floured pastry board. Using the large petal cutters, stamp out about 24 petals for each flower and using the canapé cutter, one round center. Remove the excess dough and place a row of petals around each centerpiece. Pinch the points of each petal and then use a toothpick to make a groove in the center. Add a second row of petals in the same way as the first (see Leaves and flowers, page 23). Place a small ball of dough in a garlic press and scoop the resulting strands onto the center to resemble seeds.

● Transfer the flowers to the microwave turntable plate and bake on low for 10 minutes, medium low for 5 minutes + 3 minutes, and medium for 2 minutes + 1 minute. Remove them from the microwave oven and leave to cool.

● Apply two coats of white acrylic paint to both sides of each flower to act as a sealant and bottom coat. When the paint is dry, apply three coats of varnish, leaving each coat to dry before applying the next.

● Make a square frame from the wooden edging to fit the plywood backing. Glue together and then use molding pins to keep in place. Paint the frame brown. Cut a square of hessian to fit inside the frame and attach, using double-sided adhesive tape. Attach the small blocks of wood to the center of each frame using epoxy resin glue. Secure the flower on top which creates a three-dimensional effect.

Welsh Love Spoons

An age-old tradition in Wales, love spoons were carved from wood and given as love tokens, or christening gifts. Salt dough is an ideal medium for recreating similar decorative pieces using some of the traditional motifs such as hearts and twists.

YOU WILL NEED

1 batch salt dough (see page 11)
    makes three about
    10 inches long
Rolling pin
Flour
Pastry board
Tracing paper
Pencil
Plain paper
Scissors
Small knife
Small teaspoon
Modeling tools or wooden skewer
Fine grade sandpaper
Paintbrushes
Satin polyurethane varnish
Ribbons

● Roll out the dough to a thickness of ¼ inch on a lightly floured pastry board. Trace off the templates on page 122 and cut out in plain paper. Lay the complete spoon template and two spoon bowls on the rolled-out dough and cut around.

● For the complete template spoon, use the handle of a small teaspoon and your fingers to model the bowl into a dished shape (see Bowled and twisted shapes, page 21). Add any decorative detail, using a modeling tool or a wooden skewer. For the other spoons, model the bowl and decorate in the same way; then roll two long sausage shapes and twist to form the handle. Either bend to form heart shapes or add cutout hearts to the top. Press the spoon bowl carefully onto the base of the handle to join (see page 21). Add a small ring of dough to the top of each spoon as a hanging hole.

● Transfer the spoons to the microwave turntable plate and bake on low for 15 minutes + 10 minutes, medium low for 5 minutes + 5 minutes, and medium for 2 minutes + 2 minutes. Remove them from the oven and leave to cool. Using sandpaper, smooth off any rough edges.

● Apply three coats of satin varnish to both sides of the spoons, leaving each coat to dry before applying the next. The dough is left unpainted to create the effect of wood. Attach a pretty ribbon bow and hanging loop to each spoon.

Bead Necklace

Model a string of chunky beads, then paint and pattern them in bright summer colors to suit your mood or your outfit.

YOU WILL NEED

¼ batch salt dough (see page 11)

Rolling pin

Flour

Pastry board

Plenty of wooden skewers

Small round canapé cutter

Toothpicks

Large glass bowl

Block of florist's foam

Small paintbrushes

Acrylic paints

Satin polyurethane varnish

Fine leather thong

● Break off handfuls of dough and roll each into a sausage about the diameter of the finished bead on a lightly floured pastry board. Cut the dough with a small knife into ½-inch lengths. Roll each length into a ball and thread onto a wooden skewer. Balance the skewer over the rim of a large glass bowl (this insures that the rounded shape is not distorted during baking). Make about 30 beads in this way (see Making beads, page 23).

● Roll out the remaining dough to a thickness of ⅛ inch on a lightly floured pastry board. Using the small canapé cutter, stamp out about 40 round flat shapes. Pierce a hole through the center of each with the blunt end of a toothpick.

● Transfer the beads to the microwave turntable plate and bake on low for 10 minutes + 5 minutes, medium low for 5 minutes + 3 minutes, and medium for 2 minutes + 2 minutes. Remove the beads from the microwave oven and leave to dry.

● To decorate the beads, place each one on the end of a toothpick (this will hold the bead steady while you paint) and push the toothpick into the florist's foam in an upright position to let the paint dry. Decorate the beads, using the photograph as a guide or choose designs of your own.

● When the paint is dry, apply three coats of varnish, leaving each to dry before applying the next. Thread the beads onto a fine leather thong and tie the ends together securely.

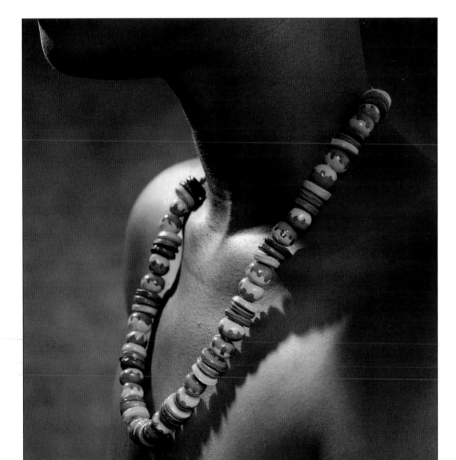

Aztec Mask

A stunning wall decoration created by molding and layering simple template shapes combined with surface texturing techniques. The earthy yellows, reds and greens blend so well together to produce a strikingly authentic effect.

YOU WILL NEED

1 batch salt dough (see page 11)

Rolling pin

Flour

Pastry board

Tracing paper

Pencil

Plain paper

Scissors

Small knife

5-inch diameter saucer to use as a
    mold

Plastic food wrap

Modeling tools

Wooden skewer

Fine grade sandpaper

Paintbrushes

Acrylic paints

Small synthetic sponge (optional)

Satin polyurethane varnish

● Roll out the dough to a thickness of ¼ inch on a lightly floured pastry board. Trace off the basic template on page 123, and then trace off the other template details following the solid lines (the dotted lines represent surface details). Cut out the templates in plain paper and place on the rolled-out dough. Cut around each shape, using a small knife, removing the eye and mouth sections. Remove the excess dough.

● Cover the convex side of the saucer with plastic food wrap and lay it on the pastry board. Carefully lift the main mask template and place it over the mold. The saucer should fit under the face part of the mask and the head-dress should lie flat on the board. Moisten the entire surface of the dough with water and carefully lay the other cutout shapes in position.

● Use modeling tools or a wooden skewer to make the surface decorations, referring to the dotted lines on the template and to the photograph as a guide. Use a moistened modeling tool to smooth out the joins. The raised details on the forehead and earrings are made from small balls of dough squashed to make a flatter shape and then pierced with the blunt end of a skewer. For the nose, model a small ball of dough into a pyramid shape and press it carefully into position, smoothing out the joins with a moistened modeling tool. Form the nostrils, using a pointed modeling tool.

● Transfer the mask to the microwave turntable plate and bake on low for 20 minutes + 20 minutes, medium low for 20 minutes, and medium for 10 minutes + 10 minutes. Remove it from the microwave oven and leave to cool. Do not attempt to remove the mold while the dough is still warm as this may cause warping and damage. Gently prize the dough mask away from the mold and, using sandpaper, smooth off any rough edges.

● Apply two coats of beige acrylic paint to both sides of the mask to act as a sealant and bottom coat. Apply the other decorative colors, using the photograph as a guide. Use a dry brush or a sponge to achieve the subtle effects.

● When the decorative paintwork is dry, apply three coats of varnish, leaving each coat to dry before applying the next.

Rose Wreath

This decorative piece with textured leaves and rose buds was inspired by the modeled bread dough wreaths made in Crete. The tradition of bread dough modeling is one that dates back to ancient times – this particular example translates well into salt dough form and is not as complicated to make as it looks.

YOU WILL NEED

1 batch salt dough (see page 11)

Rolling pin

Flour

Pastry board

Plain paper

Pencil

Scissors

Small knife

Small leaf-shaped cookie cutters

Fork

Toothpick or fine modeling tool

Paintbrush

Satin polyurethane varnish

● Roll out the dough to a thickness of ¼ inch on a lightly floured pastry board. Cut out a 9-inch diameter round in plain paper to use as a template for the base. Cut another round about 5 inches from the center. Place the paper ring on the rolled-out dough and cut around it with a small knife.

● Gather up the excess dough and reroll to the same thickness. Using a cookie cutter, stamp out plenty of rounded leaf shapes and press the tines of a fork firmly into the surface to make deep grooves. Press the leaves around the outside and inside circumference of the dough ring. Cut out a large number of pointed leaf shapes. Using a toothpick or a fine modeling tool, trace on the veins. Place these leaves on the dough ring just inside the first rows. For the rose buds, cut out an oval leaf shape and press flat. Roll up the flat shape to form the flower. Place the flowers in groups of three or four around the ring. Fill in any gaps with tiny rose buds or leaves (see Leaves and flowers, page 23).

● Transfer the wreath to the microwave turntable plate and bake on low for 30 minutes + 30 minutes, medium low for 15 minutes + 15 minutes + 15 minutes, and medium for 10 minutes + 5 minutes + 5 minutes. Remove the wreath from the microwave oven and leave to cool.

● Apply three coats of satin varnish to both sides of the wreath, leaving each coat to dry before applying the next. This particular model has been left unpainted to show the natural color of the dough. It is important, however, to make sure that all the convoluted surfaces of the shape are completely sealed with varnish.

Deep Sea Dish

*The subtlety of the blue and gold shades combined with the delicate shapes of
starfish and shells used to decorate the dish create a wonderful effect that
reflects the beauty of the undersea world.*

YOU WILL NEED

1 batch salt dough (see page 11)

Rolling pin

Flour

Pastry board

Ceramic dinner plate to use
    as a mold

Plastic food wrap

Small knife

Modeling tools

Toothpick

Epoxy resin adhesive

Paintbrushes

Acrylic paints

Gold metallic acrylic paint

Flat mixing palette

Sponge

Polyurethane varnish

● Roll out the dough to a thickness of ¼ inch on a lightly floured pastry board.
Cover the concave side of the plate with plastic food wrap to prevent the dough
from sticking. Carefully lift the rolled-out dough and place it on the plate,
pressing it into place with your fingers so the dough follows the concave shape.
Trim around the edge of the plate, using a small knife, and smooth out the cut
edge with your fingers or a moistened modeling tool.

● For the starfish, gather up the excess dough and reroll a little thinner than
before. Cut out about 15 small five-pointed star shapes, using a small knife.
Pinch each point between your thumb and forefinger. Add the textured detail
with the point of a toothpick or a fine modeling tool (see Adding surface
textures, page 19). Moisten the rim of the dish with a little water and press the
starfish shapes onto the surface. For the seaweed, cut narrow pointed strips and
press onto the surface. For the shells, gather up the remaining dough and roll
into sausage shapes, tapered at one end. Roll up from the narrow end to form
the shell. For the limpets, model a small ball of dough into shallow cone shape
and, using a toothpick, add the decorative lines.

● Transfer the plate mold to the microwave turntable plate. Place the shells
and limpets on the oven plate separately and bake on low for 20 minutes +
20 minutes, medium low for 10 minutes + 10 minutes, and medium for 5 minutes
+ 5 minutes + 5 minutes. Remove from the microwave oven and leave to cool.
Do not remove the plate mold while the dough is warm as this may cause
damage and warping. When completely dry, prize the bottom plate away from
the mold with a small knife. Using sandpaper, smooth off any rough edges.

● Attach the dough shells in place, using strong epoxy resin adhesive. When
the adhesive has set, apply two coats of light blue acrylic paint to both sides of
the dish to act as a sealant and bottom coat. Use a sponge to apply darker colors
to the outside and underside of the dish in a mottled subtle pattern and richer
mid blues to the center and to accentuate the curves of the shells. Paint the
starfish gold and apply a delicate gold blush with a sponge to the rest of
the dish.

● When the decorative paintwork is dry, apply three coats of satin varnish,
leaving each coat to dry before applying the next.

Floral Picture Frame

*A pretty frame for your favorite photograph or picture. The mock woven detail
is easily achieved by using the simplest of modeling tools, while the flowers
need a combination of cutters and modeling techniques.*

YOU WILL NEED

1 batch salt dough (see page 11)

Rolling pin

Flour

Pastry board

Pencil

Ruler

Plain paper

Scissors

Small sharp knife

Modeling tools

Different shaped small cutters –
    such as leaves and flowers

Toothpick

Wooden skewer

Fine grade sandpaper

Paintbrushes

Acrylic paint

Satin polyurethane varnish

Thin card

Transparent acetate film

Double-sided adhesive tape

Double-sided adhesive pads or
    epoxy resin adhesive

● Roll out the dough to a thickness of ¼ inch on a lightly floured pastry board. Cut out a rectangle or square in plain paper, about 1 inch larger than your picture or photograph, then cut out a window for the center that is about ⅜ inch smaller than the photograph. Lay the paper template on the rolled-out dough and, using a sharp knife, cut out the window first and then cut around the outside. Gather up the excess dough and save for later.

● Using a fine pointed modeling tool, make two long grooves along each side of the frame. Make the grooves quite deep so the detail holds. When you reach the corners, use the tool to suggest the woven details.

● Reroll the excess dough a little thinner than before. Using the small cutters, stamp out a variety of flower and leaf shapes. Moisten two diagonally opposite corners of the frame with water and press the shapes in place. Add fine details with a toothpick or modeling tool. Add flower centers by rolling a tiny ball and pressing it in place with the blunt end of a wooden skewer to make a small hole.

● Transfer the frame to the microwave turntable plate and bake on low for 20 minutes + 20 minutes, medium low for 10 minutes + 10 minutes, and medium for 2 minutes + 2 minutes + 2 minutes. Remove it from the microwave oven and leave to cool. Using sandpaper, smooth off any rough edges.

● Apply two coats of a light cream acrylic paint to both sides of the dough frame to act as a sealant and bottom coat. Paint the leaves and flowers. When the paint is dry, apply three coats of satin varnish, leaving each coat to dry before applying the next.

● To make the backing, cut out a piece of thin card and a piece of acetate the same size as the frame. Using double-sided adhesive tape, attach the acetate to the card around three edges only, leaving the lower edge free to insert the picture. Attach the backing to the reverse side of the frame with double-sided sticky pads or epoxy resin adhesive.

MODELING

Underwater World Wall Decoration

*Create a charming school of realistic sea horses that float elegantly on fronds
of seaweed, using a combination of free modeling techniques and a simple
template. Color your decoration with muted shades of green and a subtle
hint of gold.*

YOU WILL NEED

1 batch salt dough (see page 11)
Rolling pin
Flour
Pastry board
Tracing paper
Pencil
Scissors
Plain paper
Small knife
Modeling tools
Wooden skewer
Fine grade sandpaper
Paintbrushes
Acrylic paints
Gold metallic paint
Sponge
Flat mixing palette
Epoxy resin adhesive
Satin polyurethane varnish

● Roll out the dough to a thickness of ¼ inch on a lightly floured pastry board. Trace off the sea horse and seaweed templates on page 123. Cut out the shapes in plain paper and lay the templates on the rolled-out dough. Using a small knife, cut around the templates and remove the excess dough. Round off the edges of the seaweed shape with your fingers or a modeling tool moistened with water. Use two small modeling tools with flat rounded blades to pinch the dough into little peaks along the back of the sea horses. You may have to practice a little. If you make a mistake, simply reroll the dough and start again. For the eye, roll a small ball of dough, press into place, and pierce the center with the blunt end of a wooden skewer.

● Transfer the dough pieces to the microwave turntable plate and bake on low for 20 minutes + 20 minutes, medium low for 10 minutes + 10 minutes, and medium for 5 minutes + 5 minutes + 2 minutes. Because the sea horses are smaller than the seaweed shape, they will probably be ready sooner, if so remove and continue baking the larger piece. Remove the pieces from the microwave oven when dry and leave to cool. Using sandpaper, smooth off any rough edges.

● Apply two coats of acrylic paint to both sides of the dry dough shapes as a sealant and bottom coat. Color the seaweed green and the sea horses gold.

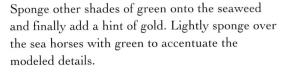

Sponge other shades of green onto the seaweed and finally add a hint of gold. Lightly sponge over the sea horses with green to accentuate the modeled details.

● When the decorative paintwork is dry, apply three coats of varnish, leaving each coat to dry before applying the next. Use epoxy resin adhesive to attach the sea horses to the seaweed shape.

Sun and Moon Bookends

Plain wooden bookends are given a celestial touch with silvery crescent moons
set on a background of the sun's golden flames.

YOU WILL NEED

1 batch salt dough (see page 11)

Rolling pin

Flour

Pastry board

Tracing paper

Pencil

Plain paper

Scissors

Small knife

Modeling tool

Wooden skewer

Fine grade sandpaper

Sheet of newspaper

Paintbrush

Gold and silver metallic
    acrylic spray paints

Satin polyurethane varnish

Approximate 2-foot length of
    2½-inch wide softwood

Small hacksaw

Hammer

Small nails

Epoxy resin adhesive

● Roll out the dough to a thickness of ¼ inch on a lightly floured pastry board. Trace off the sun and moon templates on page 124. Cut out two of each shape in plain paper and place the templates on the rolled-out dough. Cut around the templates, using a small knife.

● For the suns, pinch each pointed flame shape between your thumb and forefinger to make rounded edges and then bend each a little to resemble flickering flames. For the moons, round off the outside edge, using your fingers or a moistened modeling tool. Using the photograph and design lines suggested on the template, build up the features, using modeling tools and small pieces of dough on the moistened surface of the moon. The eyebrows and lips are thin tapered sausages of dough. Form the eyes by pressing a ball of dough into position and then make a hole in the center with the blunt end of a wooden skewer. The eyelids are a semicircle of dough pressed into place with a modeling tool.

● Transfer the suns and the moons in pairs to the microwave turntable plate and bake on low for 30 minutes + 30 minutes, medium low for 20 minutes, and medium for 5 minutes + 5 minutes + 5 minutes. Remove the shapes from the microwave oven and leave to cool. Using sandpaper, smooth off any rough edges.

● Place the dry dough shapes on a sheet of newspaper and apply two coats of acrylic spray paint to each side. Color the moons silver and the suns gold.

● When the paint is dry, apply three coats of satin varnish to both sides of each shape, leaving each coat to dry before applying the next.

● To make the bookends, cut four pieces of wood about 5 inches long and then using epoxy resin glue, stick together to form two right angles. Cut two small triangles from the remaining wood and glue in position to support the angles. When the glue has set, nail the wooden pieces together securely and spray with gold acrylic paint.

● Use epoxy resin adhesive to attach first the sun to the support triangle of each bookend and then the moons on top.

Tulip Key Holder

Tulips and tiny forget-me-nots give this pretty wall decoration a fresh
springtime feel. Not only attractive but functional too, the terracotta colored
base has a row of tiny hooks to keep your house keys safe.

YOU WILL NEED

½ batch salt dough (see page 11)

Rolling pin

Flour

Pastry board

Tracing paper

Pencil

Plain paper

Scissors

Small knife

Small flower- and leaf-shaped
  cutters

Garlic press

Wooden skewer

Paintbrushes

Acrylic paint

Sponge

Satin polyurethane varnish

Hand drill with small bit

Small brass screw-in hooks

● Roll out the dough to a thickness of ¼ inch on a lightly floured pastry board. Trace off the templates for the base and leaves on page 124 and cut out in plain paper. Lay on the rolled-out dough and cut around the base template, using a small knife. Then cut out about 12 large leaf shapes and about 8 smaller ones. Remove the excess dough and reroll a little thinner than before. Using small cutters, stamp out more leaf shapes and some forget-me-nots.

● Place the large leaves in a row growing up from the top of the base. Pinch the pointed end of each and curve each one slightly for a more realistic effect. Do the same with the smaller leaves, placing them over the bottoms of the first. Put a small ball of dough into a garlic press and arrange the resulting strands of dough around the bottom of the leaves to resemble moss. Add some more small leaves, making the veins with a modeling tool, and then add some tiny forget-me-nots, piercing the center of each with the blunt end of a wooden skewer. Roll small balls of dough into egg shapes for the tulip blooms. Place these on the leafy background and roll very thin sausage shapes to act as stems for each bloom.

● Transfer the model to the microwave turntable plate and bake on low for 15 minutes + 15 minutes, medium low for 10 minutes + 5 minutes, and medium for 3 minutes + 3 minutes + 3 minutes. Remove it from the microwave oven and leave to cool. Using sandpaper, smooth off any rough edges.

● Apply two coats of acrylic paint to both sides of the model as a sealant and bottom coat. Color the leaves and flowers green and the base terracotta. Follow the photograph as a guide and use your imagination for the other decorative details. Sponge on a light sheen of cream-colored paint to highlight the modeled shapes.

● When the decorative paintwork is dry, apply three coats of varnish, leaving each coat to dry before applying the next.

● Finally, drill four small holes at the bottom of the model and screw in the brass hooks.

Winged Heart Hat Pins

Pretty winged hearts to add a touch of style and color to a winter hat. The feathers are quite finely detailed and offer an excellent opportunity to practice new modeling skills.

YOU WILL NEED

¼ batch salt dough (see page 11)
Rolling pin
Flour
Pastry board
Tracing paper
Pencil
Plain paper
Scissors
Small knife
Modeling tools
Toothpick
Modeling syringe
Wooden skewer
Fine grade sandpaper
Paintbrushes
Acrylic paint
Small synthetic sponge
Silver and gold metallic
    acrylic paints
Satin polyurethane varnish
Hat pins
Strong epoxy resin adhesive

● Roll out the dough to a thickness of ¼ inch on a lightly floured pastry board. Trace off the basic heart, wing and feather templates on page 125. Trace the heart shapes (tinted pink on the templates) out again. Cut out in plain paper and place on top of the rolled-out dough. Cut around the templates, using a small knife. Remove the excess dough and reroll to a thickness of ⅛ inch.

● Using a modeling tool, cut out the elongated feather shapes (you may be able to find a small cake decorator's cutter that matches the shape). Moisten the wing shapes with a little water and lay the feather shapes on top, one row at a time. Using a toothpick, make a groove down the center of each feather and smaller grooves radiating from it. Place a small ball of well-kneaded dough into a modeling syringe and extrude a fine string down the central groove to form the spine. Do this for each feather and then lay on the next row.

● Finally, press the cutout heart shapes into position, covering the ends of the feathers and making neat centers. For the smaller hat pins, use the blunt end of a wooden skewer to make a pattern of small dots around the inside of the heart shapes.

● Transfer the hearts to the microwave turntable plate and bake on low for 10 minutes + 10 minutes, medium low for 5 minutes + 5 minutes, and medium for 2 minutes + 2 minutes. Remove them from the microwave oven and leave to cool. Using sandpaper, smooth off any rough edges.

● Apply two coats of acrylic paint to the dough shape to act as a sealant and bottom coat, coloring the heart pink and the wings gray or cream. Sponge some gold paint onto the wings and silver to the heart to accentuate the modeled details.

● When the paint has dried, apply three coats of polyurethane varnish, leaving each coat to dry before applying the next.

● Attach the ends of the hat pins to the reverse side of the dough shapes, using a strong epoxy resin adhesive.

Scrolled Mirror Frame

*These elegant, swirling scrolls, created by simple but effective free modeling
techniques, add a touch of sophistication to an otherwise plain mirror.*

YOU WILL NEED

¼ batch salt dough (see page 11)

Rolling pin

Flour

Pastry board

Tracing paper

Pencil

Plain paper

Scissors

Small knife

Fine grade sandpaper

Paintbrushes

Acrylic paint

Gold metallic acrylic paint

Small synthetic sponge

Satin polyurethane varnish

Small mirror with stand (about
    4 x 6 inches)

Double-sided adhesive pads

● Roll out the dough to a thickness of ¼ inch on a lightly floured pastry board. Trace off the base template on page 125. Cut out in plain paper and place on the rolled-out dough. Cut around the template, using a small knife.

● Gather up the remaining dough. Break off small balls and roll into sausage shapes, tapered at both ends, about ⅜ inch in diameter and about 4 inches long. Pinch each sausage shape along the length between your thumb and forefinger to make a pointed ridge, then roll up the shape from both ends to form an "S." Moisten the surface of the base with water and press the "S" shapes into position. Make smaller swirls to fill in any gaps (see Free modeling, page 22).

● Transfer the dough frame to the microwave turntable plate and bake on low for 15 minutes + 10 minutes, medium for 10 minutes + 5 minutes, and medium for 3 minutes + 3 minutes. Remove the frame from the microwave oven and leave to cool. Using sandpaper, smooth off any roughness.

● Apply two coats of white acrylic paint to both sides of the frame as a sealant and bottom coat. Sponge on a little gold to accentuate the swirling contours.

● When the decorative paintwork is dry, apply three coats of varnish to both sides of the frame, leaving each coat to dry before applying the next.

● Paint the small mirror's frame to match the dough frame and attach it to the back of the dough frame with double-sided adhesive pads when the varnish has dried.

4

DECORATIVE PIECES

Fringed Lamp Shade

*A plain lamp shade can be given an unusual decorative touch by suspending
flat triangular dough shapes from the bottom.*

YOU WILL NEED

¼ batch salt dough (see page 11)

Rolling pin

Flour

Pastry board

Tracing paper

Pencil

Plain paper

Scissors

Small knife

Toothpick

Fine grade sandpaper

Paintbrushes

Acrylic paints

Satin polyurethane varnish

Bodkin

Fine black cord or colored string

Lamp and lamp shade

● Roll out the dough to a thickness of ¼ inch on a lightly floured pastry board. Trace off the template shape given on page 126 and cut out as many shapes as you need in plain paper. Place the templates on the rolled-out dough and cut around each one, using a small knife. Remove the excess dough. Round off the edges of each shape with your fingers and pierce a small hole at the top, using a toothpick.

● Transfer the shapes to the microwave turntable plate and bake on low for 10 minutes + 10 minutes and medium low for 5 minutes + 5 minutes. Remove the shapes from the microwave oven and leave to cool. Using sandpaper, smooth off any rough edges.

● Apply two coats of light colored acrylic paint to both sides of each shape to act as a sealant and bottom coat. Then paint on a contrasting color and any details, using the photograph as a guide or choosing your own patterns.

● When the decorative paintwork is dry, apply three coats of varnish, leaving each coat to dry before applying the next.

● Using a bodkin, pierce a row of small holes through the lamp shade around the bottom. Tie on each shape with a small piece of fine cord or colored string.

Vegetable Pots

Terracotta flower pots covered with rough jute string provide a natural-looking base for simple vegetable decorations. Use the pots for storage or for keeping kitchen implements tidy.

YOU WILL NEED

⅛ batch salt dough (see page 11)

Rolling pin

Flour

Pastry board

Tracing paper

Pencil

Plain paper

Scissors

Small knife

Toothpick

Fine grade sandpaper

Paintbrushes

Acrylic paints

Satin polyurethane varnish

Straight-sided terracotta
    flower pots

Craft adhesive

Ball of natural jute string

Epoxy resin adhesive

● Roll out the dough to a thickness of ⅛ inch on a lightly floured pastry board. Trace off the chili pepper, carrot and scallion templates given on page 126. Cut out each shape in plain paper and place on the rolled-out dough. Cut around each shape, using a small knife. Remove the excess dough. Round off the edges of the shapes with your fingers and add a little surface detail to the scallion and the carrot with a toothpick.

● Transfer the shapes to the microwave turntable plate and bake on low for 10 minutes + 10 minutes and medium low for 5 minutes + 5 minutes. Remove the shapes from the oven and leave to cool. Using sandpaper, smooth off any rough edges.

● Apply two coats of light colored acrylic paint to both sides of the shapes to act as a sealant and bottom coat. Using the photograph as a guide, paint on the main colors and details.

● When the decorative paintwork is dry, apply three coats of varnish, leaving each coat to dry before applying the next.

● Using a brush, cover the outside of the flower pots with craft adhesive. Leave the glue to become tacky and then, beginning at the bottom of each pot, wind the jute string around the pot pressing it into the adhesive. Attach the dough vegetables to the pots, using epoxy resin adhesive.

Sunflower Hat

Trim a summer straw hat with a vibrant ring of sunflowers.

YOU WILL NEED

¼ batch salt dough (see page 11)

Rolling pin

Flour

Pastry board

Assorted-size leaf end circular
    cutters

Modeling tool or toothpick

Garlic press

Fine grade sandpaper

Paintbrushes

Acrylic paint

Satin polyurethane varnish

Double-sided adhesive pads

Straw hat

● Roll out the dough to a thickness of ¼ inch on a lightly floured pastry board. Use the cutters to stamp out one circular center, about 24 petal shapes and two or three leaves for each flower. Remove the excess dough.

● Place the circular center on the pastry board and two or three leaves radiating from it. Arrange 12 petals around the center and, using a modeling tool or toothpick, make an indentation at the bottom of each to attach to the center and to create detail. Add another row of petals in the same way (see Leaves and flowers, page 23). Put a small ball of dough into a garlic press and scoop the resulting strands onto the center to form a seeded texture. Make as many flowers as you need in the same way.

● Transfer the flowers to the microwave turntable plate and bake on low for 10 minutes + 10 minutes, medium low for 5 minutes + 5 minutes, and medium for 2 minutes. Remove them from the microwave oven and leave to cool. Using sandpaper, smooth off any rough edges.

● Apply two coats of yellow acrylic paint to both sides of the flowers to act as a sealant and bottom coat. Then apply darker greens for the leaves and any other decorative details. When the decorative paintwork is dry, apply three coats of varnish, leaving each coat to dry before applying the next.

● Use double-sided adhesive pads to attach the flowers to the straw hat.

Mexican Candlesticks

Lizards and firebirds are typical design motifs of Ancient Mexico. The stylized, uncomplicated outlines lend themselves very well to template work. Paint matt black and then add a spattering of gold to create a burnished appearance.

YOU WILL NEED

¼ batch salt dough (see page 11)

Rolling pin

Flour

Pastry board

Tracing paper

Pencil

Plain paper

Scissors

Small knife

Modelling tools

Fine grade sandpaper

Paintbrushes

Acrylic paint

Pair of candlesticks

Sheet of newspaper

Gold metallic acrylic spray paint

Satin polyurethane varnish

Strong epoxy resin adhesive

● Roll out the dough to a thickness of ¼ inch on a lightly floured pastry board. Trace off the lizard and firebird templates on page 126. Trace the relief decorations (the areas tinted cream) separately. Cut out each shape in plain paper and place on the rolled-out dough. Cut around the shapes, using a small knife, and remove the excess dough. Moisten the surface of the main shapes with water and gently press the relief decorations into position. Using a modeling tool, smooth out the joins.

● Transfer the shapes to the microwave turntable plate and bake on low for 15 minutes and medium low for 5 minutes. Remove them from the microwave oven and leave to cool. Using sandpaper, smooth off any rough edges.

● Apply two coats of black acrylic paint to both sides of the shapes to act as a sealant and bottom coat. Paint the candlesticks black too (acrylic paints are very versatile and will adhere to most surfaces including metals and plastics). Then place the candlesticks and dough pieces on a sheet of newspaper and lightly spray with gold metallic paint.

● When the decorative paintwork is dry, apply three coats of varnish, leaving each coat to dry before applying the next. Attach the decorations to the candlestick stems, using epoxy resin adhesive.

Candle Motifs

*Perfect as a small gift or token, pairs of colored candles, each wrapped with a
band of card or ribbon and embellished with a matching star. Use different
motifs or color schemes to suit the season or occasion, such as Christmas,
Mother's Day or Easter.*

YOU WILL NEED

Small quantity salt dough
   (see page 11)
Rolling pin
Flour
Pastry board
Star-shaped cookie cutter
Small round canapé cutter
Small knife
Modeling tool
Paintbrushes
Acrylic paint
Sheet of newspaper
Toothbrush
Flat mixing palette
Gold metallic acrylic spray paint
Satin polyurethane varnish
Matching colored card or ribbon
Epoxy resin adhesive
Colored candles

● Roll out the dough to a thickness of ¼ inch on a lightly floured pastry board. Using the star-shaped cutter, stamp out as many shapes as you need. Cut a circular hole from the center of each star. Remove the round of dough and trim it a little smaller, using a small knife. With a pointed modeling tool, mark the spiral-shaped pattern onto the surface of the dough.

● Transfer the shapes to the microwave turntable plate and bake on low for 5 minutes + 5 minutes and medium low for 2 minutes + 2 minutes. Remove the shapes from the microwave oven and leave to cool.

● Apply two coats of acrylic paint to both sides of the shapes to act as a sealant and bottom coat. Place the painted shapes on a sheet of newspaper and, using a toothbrush dipped in a watery solution of gold metallic paint, add the speckled decoration. Draw the blade of a knife toward you across the bristles, which will deposit tiny spots of paint on the dough shapes (see Finishing, painting and decorative effects, page 25).

● When the decorative paintwork is dry, apply three coats of varnish, leaving each coat to dry before applying the next.

● Attach each shape to a band of colored card or ribbon, using epoxy resin adhesive, and wrap around the candles.

Seashore Boxes

Salt dough clam shells and starfish, in addition to being attractive as freestanding ornaments, make pretty decorations for small boxes. Paint the shells a crisp white and then add hints of pale pastel shades.

YOU WILL NEED

¼ batch salt dough (see page 11)
Rolling pin
Flour
Pastry board
Tracing paper
Pencil
Plain paper
Scissors
Small knife
Toothpick
Fine grade sandpaper
Paintbrushes
Acrylic paints
Sponge
Flat mixing palette
Satin polyurethane varnish
Small wooden boxes
Strong epoxy resin adhesive

● Roll out the dough to a thickness of ¼ inch on a lightly floured pastry board. Trace out the shell and starfish templates on page 126. Cut out the shapes in plain paper and place on top of the rolled-out dough. Cut around the templates, using a small knife, and remove the excess dough.

● Pinch the fish shapes between your thumb and forefinger and bend each one slightly to form a more pleasing shape. Then make rows of small dots, using the point of a toothpick. For the clam shells, use a toothpick to make grooves radiating from the bottom outward.

● Transfer the dough shapes to the microwave turntable plate and bake on low for 15 minutes + 15 minutes and medium low for 10 minutes + 5 minutes. Remove the shapes from the microwave oven and leave to cool. Using sandpaper, smooth off any rough edges.

● Apply two coats of white acrylic paint to both sides of the shapes to act as a sealant and bottom coat. Then sponge on a hint of pastel colors to accentuate the modeled details.

● When the decorative paintwork is dry, apply three coats of varnish, leaving each coat to dry before applying the next.

● Paint the wooden boxes with a wash of matching pastel color. When dry, attach a dough shape to each lid, using epoxy resin adhesive.

Celestial Bottle Stoppers

Vibrant cobalt blue glass bottles are perfectly complemented by silver-colored star and moon decorations. The salt dough shapes are simply attached to small pieces of wire and inserted into the cork bottle stopper.

YOU WILL NEED

⅛ batch salt dough (see page 11)

Rolling pin

Flour

Pastry board

Star- and moon-shaped
    cookie cutters

Fine grade sandpaper

Colored glass bottles with
    cork stoppers

Sheet of newspaper

Silver metallic acrylic spray paint

Paintbrush

Satin polyurethane varnish

Wire cutter

Wire coat hanger

Epoxy resin adhesive

● Roll out the dough to a thickness of ¼ inch on a lightly floured pastry board. Using the cookie cutters, stamp out the star and moon shapes. Remove the excess dough and, using your fingers, gently round off the edges of the shapes.

● Transfer to the microwave turntable plate and bake on low for 10 minutes + 5 minutes and medium low for 5 minutes. Remove the shapes from the microwave oven and leave to cool. Using sandpaper, smooth off any rough edges.

● Place the shapes and the cork stoppers on a sheet of newspaper and spray with silver metallic acrylic paint. When the paint is dry, apply three coats of varnish to the dough shapes, leaving each coat to dry before applying the next.

● Cut three 4-inch lengths of wire from a coat hanger. Bend one end of each into a small loop and attach to the reverse side of the dough shape, using strong epoxy resin adhesive. When the adhesive has set hard, push the wires into the corks.

Bead Bags

*Salt dough beads and buttons painted in this colorful ethnic-style cheer up
plain cotton drawstring bags. Remember to remove the decorations if you want
to wash the bags.*

YOU WILL NEED
Small quantity salt dough
　(see page 11)
Flour
Pastry board
Wooden skewers
Large glass bowl
Bodkin
Toothpicks
Block of florist's foam
Paintbrushes
Acrylic paint
Satin polyurethane varnish
Needle and thread
Drawstring bags

● For the beads, roll the dough into a sausage about ⅜ inch in diameter on a lightly floured pastry board. Cut into small sections, roll each one into a ball, and thread onto a skewer. Balance the skewer over a glass bowl (this prevents the rounded shape from becoming distorted during baking, see page 23). For the buttons, roll small balls of dough and flatten to form the button shape. Pierce two small holes in each, using a bodkin or toothpick.

● Transfer to the microwave turntable plate and bake on low for 10 minutes + 5 minutes and medium low for 5 minutes + 3 minutes. Remove the shapes from the microwave oven and leave to cool.

● Apply two coats of acrylic paint to both sides of the shapes to act as a sealant and bottom coat. Use toothpicks stuck into florist's foam to support the beads while painting and varnishing. When the decorative paintwork is dry, apply three coats of varnish, leaving each coat to dry before applying the next.

● Stitch the buttons onto the front of the bags and thread the beads onto the drawstrings, securing with a knot.

Jeweled Boxes

Luxurious golden gift boxes topped with six-pointed jeweled stars, imaginative gift containers or if you cannot bear to give them away, use them for keeping jewelry or trinkets.

YOU WILL NEED

½ batch salt dough (see page 11)

Rolling pin

Flour

Pastry board

Tracing paper

Pencil

Plain paper

Scissors

Small knife

Modeling tool

Fine grade sandpaper

Sheet of newspaper

Gold metallic acrylic spray paint

Paintbrushes

Acrylic paints

Satin polyurethane varnish

Plain gift boxes

Epoxy resin adhesive

● Roll out the dough to a thickness of ¼ inch on a lightly floured pastry board. Trace off the templates on page 127. Cut out each shape in plain paper and place each on the rolled-out dough. Cut around each shape carefully, using a small knife.

● Gather up the excess dough and roll into thin sausage shapes. Place one around the center edge of each star. Smooth out the join, using a moistened modeling tool. Roll lots of small balls from the remaining dough and press into position around the center rims and at the ends of each point.

● Transfer the shapes to the microwave turntable plate and bake on low for 20 minutes + 10 minutes and medium low for 5 minutes + 5 minutes. Remove the shapes from the microwave oven and leave to cool. Using sandpaper, smooth off any rough edges.

● Lay the dough shapes on a large sheet of newspaper and apply two coats of gold acrylic spray paint to both sides to act as a sealant and bottom coat. Paint the balls at the end of each point in rich jewel colors. Spray the boxes gold.

● When the decorative paintwork is dry, apply three coats of varnish, leaving each coat to dry before applying the next.

● Attach the decorative stars to the box lids, using epoxy resin adhesive.

Seashell Drawer Knobs

This old miniature chest has been given a new lease of life with a lick of paint and some shell-shaped knobs. So simple and yet very effective, you can add dough decorations to any flat surface.

YOU WILL NEED

⅛ batch salt dough (see page 11)

Flour

Pastry board

Small knife

Paintbrushes

Acrylic paint

Small synthetic sponge

Latex emulsion paint

Flat mixing palette

Satin polyurethane varnish

Epoxy resin adhesive

Plain drawer handles with a
    flat top

Small drawer chest

● Break the dough into small balls and roll each into a sausage, tapered at one end and about 6 inches long and ⅜ inch in diameter at the thick end. Using a small knife, cut the untapered end straight. Roll up each sausage from the tapered end to form a shell shape for each of the drawers. Make some coil in the opposite direction.

● Transfer the shapes to the microwave turntable plate and bake on low for 10 minutes + 10 minutes and medium low for 5 minutes + 3 minutes. Remove them from the microwave oven and leave to cool.

● Apply two coats of acrylic paint to both sides of the shell shapes to act as a sealant and bottom coat. Sponge on a contrasting color to highlight the modeled detail. Paint the drawers with two coats of latex emulsion in the base color and then, mix a small amount of a contrasting color to a watery consistency and apply a thin coating using a dry brush. This gives a very subtle two-color effect.

● When the decorative paintwork is dry, apply three coats of varnish, leaving each coat to dry before applying the next.

● Attach the new dough knobs to the existing drawer handles, using epoxy resin adhesive.

Tulip Basket

Decorate a plain wicker basket with little tulip motifs painted with checks and spots for a country look.

YOU WILL NEED

⅛ batch salt dough (see page 11)

Rolling pin

Flour

Pastry board

Tracing paper

Plain paper

Pencil

Scissors

Small knife

Fine grade sandpaper

Acrylic paint

Brushes

Mixing palette

Acrylic spray paint

Newspaper

Satin polyurethane varnish

Epoxy resin adhesive

● Roll out the dough to a thickness of ¼ inch on a lightly floured pastry board.

● Trace off the tulip template given on page 127 and cut as many as you need from plain paper. Lay the templates onto the rolled out dough and cut around the outside using a sharp knife.

● Transfer to the microwave turntable plate and bake low for 10 minutes, and medium low for 5 minutes. When the dough is dry, remove from the microwave oven and allow to cool. Using sandpaper, smooth off any rough edges.

● Apply two coats of acrylic paint to both sides of the tulip shapes to act as a sealant and bottom coat. Then with a contrasting color paint, add checked and spotted details. When the decorative paintwork is dry, apply three coats of varnish, leaving each coat to dry before applying the next.

● Place the wicker basket on a large sheet of newspaper and apply one or two coats of acrylic spray paint. When the paint is dry, fix on the dough motifs using epoxy resin adhesive.

TEMPLATES AND CUTTERS

Enlarge all templates to 150% for real size

Rustic Chicken
page 28

Folk Art Gift Tags
page 33

Cupid's Arrows
page 30

Teapot Refrigerator Magnets
page 36

Palm Tree Mirror Frames
page 34
Dotted line represents mirror
Blue area represents card

Starlight Candle Holders
page 40

Bird-in-the-Bush
page 42

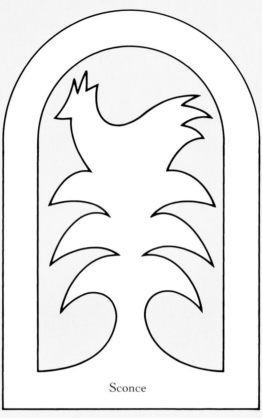

Sconce

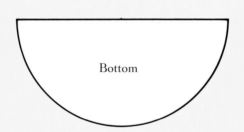

Bottom

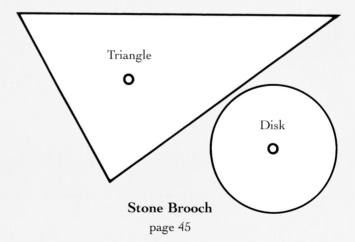

Triangle

○

Disk

○

Terracotta Earrings
page 39

Stone Brooch
page 45

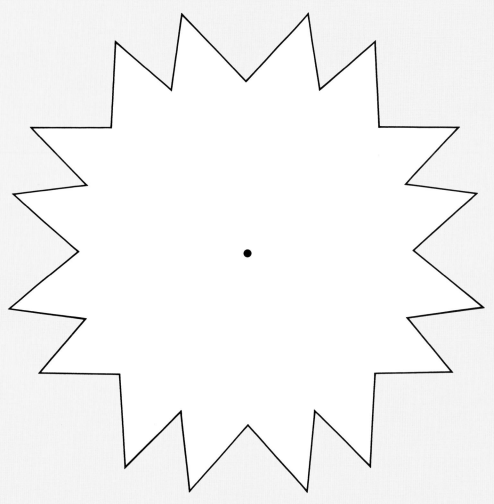

Sunburst Clock
page 48

Tropical Fish Coat Hooks
page 44

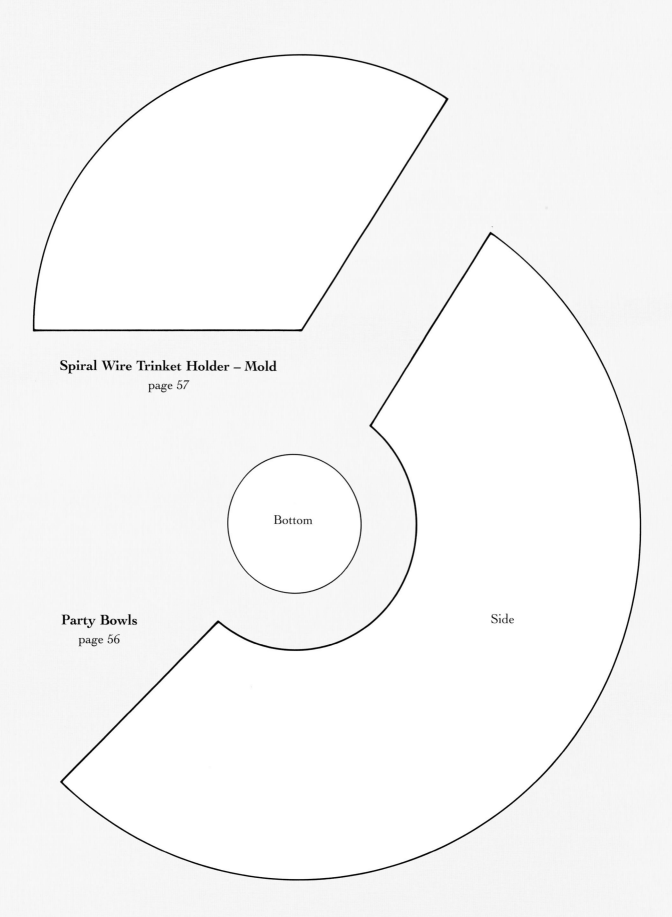

Spiral Wire Trinket Holder – Mold
page 57

Party Bowls
page 56

Bottom

Side

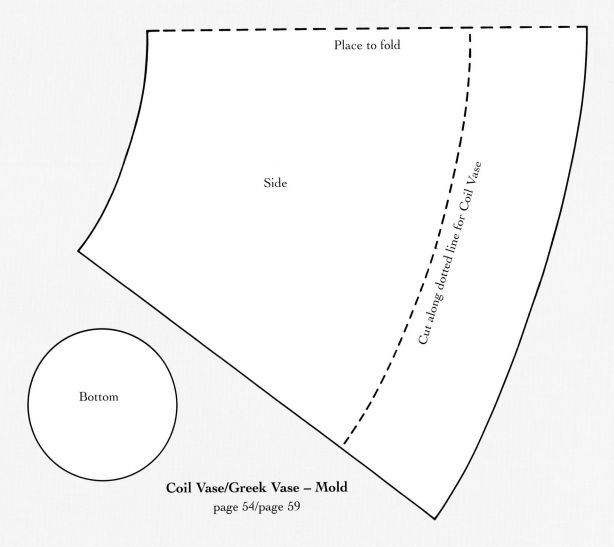

Place to fold

Side

Cut along dotted line for Coil Vase

Bottom

Coil Vase/Greek Vase – Mold
page 54/page 59

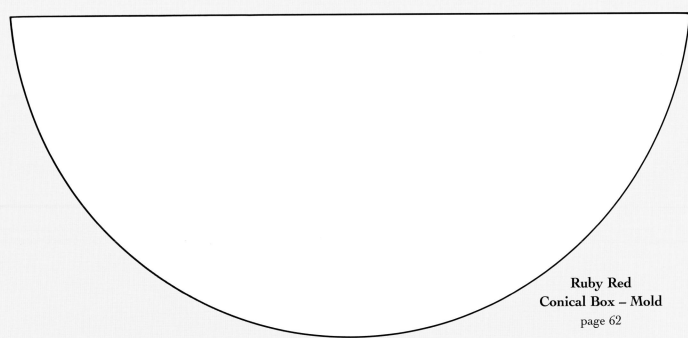

**Ruby Red
Conical Box – Mold**
page 62

Fishy Dishes
page 63
Dotted line indicates
position of saucer

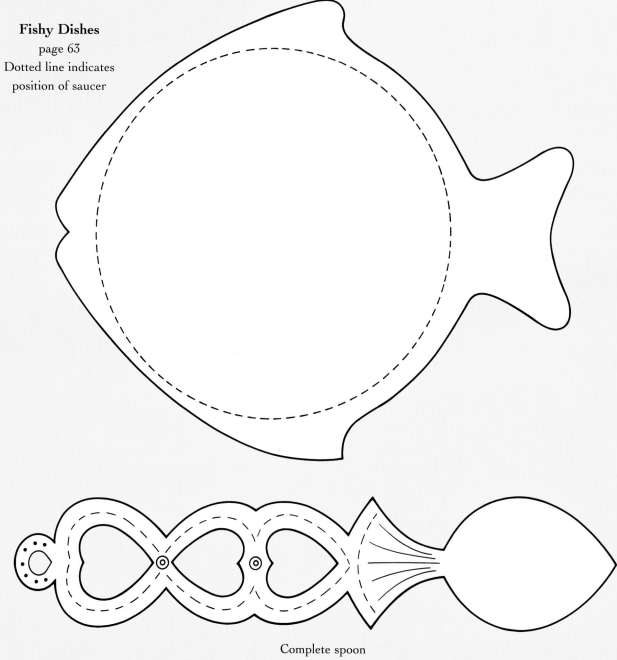

Complete spoon

Welsh Love Spoons
page 80

x 2

Spoon bowl

Aztec Mask
page 83
Dotted lines
represent
surface detail

**Underwater World
Wall Decoration**
page 89

Sea horse
x 4

Seaweed

Place to fold

Place to fold

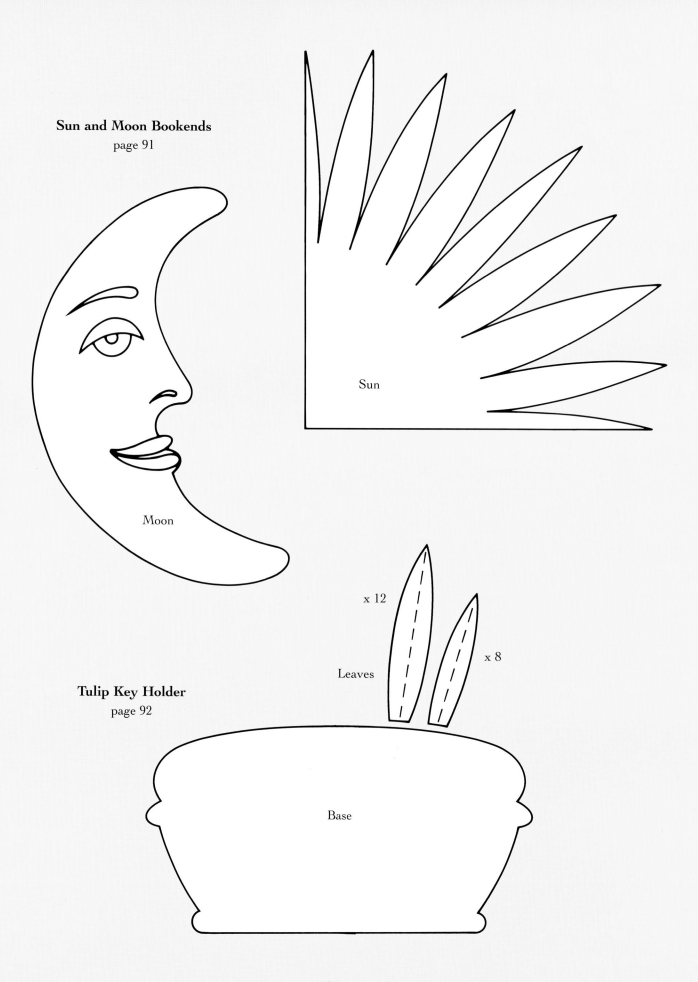

Sun and Moon Bookends
page 91

Moon

Sun

x 12

Leaves

x 8

Tulip Key Holder
page 92

Base

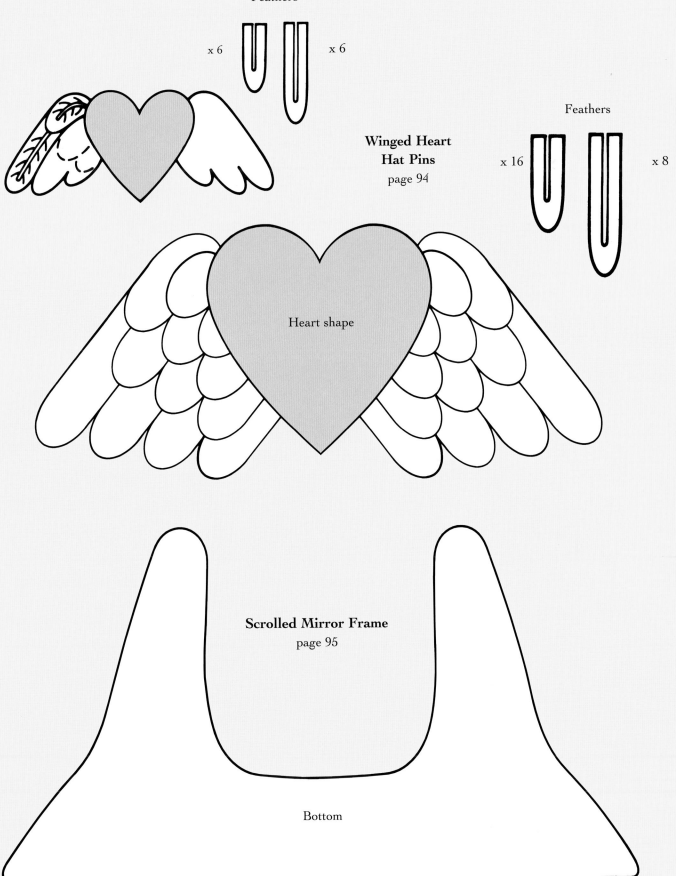

Feathers

x 6   x 6

Winged Heart Hat Pins
page 94

Feathers

x 16   x 8

Heart shape

Scrolled Mirror Frame
page 95

Bottom

Fringed Lamp Shade
page 99

Carrot

Scallion

Chili

Vegetable Pots
page 100

Lizard

Mexican Candlesticks
page 102
Areas tinted
cream represent
relief decoration

Shell

Seashore Boxes
page 106

Firebird

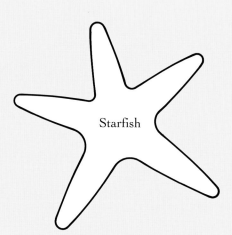

Starfish

TEMPLATES

Jeweled Boxes
page 110

Tulip Basket
page 115

Index